In Praise
of
Messy
Lives

Also by Katie Roiphe

Uncommon Arrangements
Still She Haunts Me
Last Night in Paradise
The Morning After

In Praise
of
Messy
Lives
Katie
Roiphe

CANONGATE

Edinburgh · London

Published in Great Britain in 2013 by Canongate Books Ltd,
14 High Street, Edinburgh EH1 1TE

www.canongate.tv

1

First published in the United States in 2012 by The Dial Press,
an imprint of The Random House Publishing Group,
a division of Random House, Inc., New York

This is a work of nonfiction. Some names and
identifying details have been changed.

Grateful acknowledgment is made to the following for
permission to reprint previously published material:

Grove/Atlantic, Inc.: Excerpt from "Mayakovsky" from *Meditations in an
Emergency* by Frank O'Hara, copyright © 1957 by Frank O'Hara.
Used by permission of Grove/Atlantic, Inc.

Alfred A. Knopf, a division of Random House, Inc.: Excerpt from
"Needle Biopsy" from *Endpoint and Other Poems* by John Updike,
copyright © 2009 by The Estate of John Updike. Used by permission
of Alfred A. Knopf, a division of Random House, Inc.

Every effort has been made to trace copyright holders and obtain their permission
for the use of copyright material. The publisher apologises for any errors or
omissions and would be grateful to be notified of any corrections that should
be incorporated in future reprints or editions of this book.

Previous publication information for the essays that appear in this work are
located within the author's Acknowledgments, which begin on page 263

ISBN 978 1 78211 208 2

Printed and bound in Great Britain by CPI Group (UK) Ltd, Croydon CR0 4YY

This book is printed on FSC certified paper

For Violet and Leo

Contents

PART III

The Way We Live Now

PART IV

The Internet, Etc.

Introduction

Here is something I remember from school: in French class we quickly learned that no matter what we were reading—Camus, Sartre, Ionesco, Voltaire—the correct answer to any question was always *"L'hypocrisie de la bourgeoisie."* We were good students, all girls, navy blue uniforms, and we would raise our hands and duly deliver that answer, and Madame Camille, our pretty French teacher, would smile encouragingly. I fear that same commitment to theme is a little bit on display here.

One day an editor asked me to write a piece analyzing the enormous popularity of *Mad Men,* and it was in distilling my response that I began to think about messy lives. After watching the show for a few days straight, an experience I don't necessarily recommend to anyone, it seemed to me that our conservative culture was fascinated by the spectacle of people who drank too much, smoked too much, and fell into bed with people they weren't married to, the mixed glamour of it, the stylish retrograde thrill. I began in that piece to think of messiness as a value, a good thing, a lost and interesting way of life. I had long felt discouraged by what seemed to be a certain lack of imagination in the way most of the people I knew were living, a kind of narrowness and provincialism in liberal, progressive New York circles, a cultural preoccupation with healthiness above all else, a veiled judgment toward anyone who tried to live differently; and now that discouragement felt suddenly useful and productive.

While getting my doctorate in literature, I was trained to do close readings of poems, and what I am trying to do in these essays is close readings of the outside world. I want to take apart the language we use and expose the subterranean fantasies and mythologies and assumptions at work. On disparate subjects, whether I am writing an etymology of the phrase "love child" or an analysis of the sexual preoccupations of American male novelists, I am attempting close readings of the culture. Though I have tried for the sake of neatness and clarity to divide them into sections, the line between the cultural pieces and book pieces and personal pieces is largely imaginary; they all blend and blur and spill into each other.

One review of one of my books used the colorful phrase "Roiphe-haters," and though I was a tiny bit taken aback, I am aware that there are an unusual number of people who "hate" my writing, and that I have done something to attract, if not court, that hatred. I once read someone describe me as "an uncomfortablist," which may be as accurate a characterization as any. For some probably perverse reason, I am drawn to subjects or ways of looking at things that make people, and sometimes even me, uncomfortable. In life I will go very far out of my way to avoid any possible conflict or argument, so it is a little surprising that in my essays I often seem to pick fights, and to offend or otherwise enrage people. It's hard to explain how this works, and I admit that it's fairly implausible or untenable as a way of life, but that seems to be how I go about my days: peaceably in person, fiercely on paper.

One day one of my students was doing a radio project on writers and their ideal writing conditions. He was very serious and very smart, and I would have liked to give him smart and serious answers. But I don't think I have ever had or even thought about "ideal writing conditions." I had to confess to him that my ideal writing conditions are that I have a deadline and the Con Ed bill is due.

As Virginia Woolf wrote about novels, essays and articles are not "spun in mid-air by incorporeal creatures, but are the work of suffering human beings, and are attached to grossly material things, like health and money and the houses we live in." And looking back, I can read the conditions behind some of these essays: a baby's fever, a month of not sleeping, a marriage falling apart. I am afraid the messy life is not just a theme of the essays, it's in the sentences.

In putting this collection together, it was a little surprising to me, looking at these pieces written over time, casual or serious, book pieces or culture pieces, pieces on Jane Austen or divorce, to see a pattern emerging, themes obsessively being worked through, a worldview, sometimes actively or perversely courting the extreme, and definitely not all that hugely far away from *"L'hypocrisie de la bourgeoisie."* Madame Camille, wherever she is, should be pleased.

My own life at the time of writing is a little messy. I have two children, with two different fathers, neither of whom I am living with. It did take me a little while to achieve quite this level of messiness, but I did it in the end.

I once wrote to someone: "I am kind of a failed conventional person. Or maybe my failures liberated me toward ever more colorful and flamboyant failures." And this seems as accurate a description as any of my relation to conventional life, this book being, among other things, a defense and celebration and inter-rogation of precisely those failures.

After my essay "The Naked and the Conflicted" appeared in *The New York Times Book Review*, the paper ran the following response in the letters column:

> *To the Editor:*
> *Not only are you contributing to the total annihilation of the literary culture, but also to the destruction of our civilization. Think about it.*
>
> *John Rendeiro*
> *Union, NJ*

I keep this pinned up on my office wall, for inspiration on a slow day.

PART I

Life and Times

The Great Escape

In times of trouble, some people turn to cigarettes and other people turn to drink and I read books I have read a million times before. And so in the harrowing time after I separated from my husband, I reread *The Age of Innocence*. In the early chapters, the Countess Olenska returns from Europe, having separated from her husband, and most of fashionable New York refuses to attend a dinner thrown in her honor. Even when Edith Wharton was writing, this attitude was already outdated, and yet somehow I feel a hint of it still: the same stigma mingled with fascination. I feel, suddenly, an instinctive recognition of Countess Olenska, foreign, scrutinized.

In the weeks after my husband moves out, I receive an email from someone offering to help me clean the house or cook, an email evoking images of dishes piling up in the sink, flies hovering around half-eaten peanut butter sandwiches, laundry accumulating. I wonder where these nightmarish visions of our domestic situation are coming from. Why would the departure of my husband launch me and my three-year-old, Violet, into a life of squalor? Someone else writes at around the same time: "There are no words for a catastrophe of this magnitude. I am thinking of you." And it begins to seem as if my husband has not moved five minutes away but died.

In these early days, I find telling anyone other than my closest friends about my separation a little draining, not because of my own emotions but because of theirs. One acquaintance has tears in her eyes. "Oh, my God! You poor thing. Is it *so awful* when you get home in the evening and there is no one to have dinner with? Is it *so awful* to have all those hours alone?" I am touched by her concern, but it also makes me feel like someone who has fallen off the edge of one of those colorful medieval maps to the place where there are only sea monsters and dragons. In the coming months, this tone will become familiar to me, ambient as it is of fatal illnesses. I am tempted to remind her and others of a useful line a friend drew my attention to from *As You Like It:* "Men have died from time to time, and worms have eaten them, but not for love."

Some months later, I am sitting in Bryant Park having coffee with a philosophy professor I know. It is one of those radiant early summer days when people flood out of their offices, shedding jackets and cardigans. We have both been doing research in the New York Public Library, and we are in the habit of sometimes taking a break for coffee. I am in the middle of telling him that I am finally feeling a little bit better.

"I think you are cut off from your feelings," he says. "This is a very hard time for you."

I try again. "I think maybe the worst part is over and now I am finally going to—"

"You are very fragile right now." His voice is gentle. He is going to be infinitely patient with me. "You have to take care of yourself."

And the conversation goes along in this vein. He thinks that my plan to buy a house in the next few months is "too ambitious." He thinks that the new man I am going to meet for drinks is "too soon." He thinks I am "taking on too much." Still that gentle tone of voice. Still stirring his espresso with a spoon. By the time we leave the park, I am half persuaded that I will barely make it home on the subway, since undoubtedly the ride downtown is "too much" as well. I am beginning to wonder about these expectations that I am collapsing. At no other point in my life have so many people tried so hard to convince me of how miserable I am. The professor emails my closest friend, who is a bit surprised: "I am worried about Katie." All of which reminds me that in *The Age of Innocence*, the rather powerful Countess Olenska is viewed by her peers as a "pathetic and even pitiful figure," "an exposed and pitiful figure," and "poor Ellen Olenska."

It's becoming clear to me that there is some image of the impending divorcée that I am not living up to here: hollow-eyed, bitter, harassed. Some of the more extreme sympathy I receive seems remarkably impersonal; it has less to do with me and anything I am saying than with what other people are hearing. The specifics of my experience vanish into an abstract idea about a woman's leaving a marriage. And then there seems to be a rigid script to these conversations. If I answered the question "Is it so awful to have dinner alone?" with the honest response—"Actually, sometimes I make myself a salad, and feel the stretch of the evening opening up, and reach for a book I have been wanting to read, and it is less lonely than other kinds of dinners"—it would have been almost impolite. It is counterintuitive, I know, but the true force of the loss has passed. For me, the great, unmanageable sadness came before, and this part, the starting-again part, brings along with the obvious terror its own relief.

On one of the hottest days of summer, I emerge from the train from Amagansett with Violet in my arms, both of us covered in a layer of dust, and also coated in sixteen different kinds of stickiness, including but in no way limited to a bottle of lemonade toppled on the train. Violet, meanwhile, has a cold, her nose running, in addition to pinkeye, and we are making our way home. I am balancing her on one hip and carrying our luggage with the other arm. All of a sudden, I see two very close friends bounding toward us with their giant dog, baby strapped in a Björn on the husband's chest. "How are you?" comes the inevitable question. The giant dog leaps up. Violet is terrified of the dog. She cringes into my chest. Her big bloodshot eyes emanate absolute disillusion with any hope this tattered, dissolute world has to offer. I want to say "We're fine! She's just afraid of the dog!" But then I see the tableau. We are a Walker Evans photograph of Appalachia: dirty sundresses, baby's nose running, matted hair. We are fulfilling every idea the world has of us. We are falling apart!

I once wrote an entire book about how one shouldn't reach for easy feminist interpretations of the world. And yet, even I can sense the residual sexism at work: while a woman outside of marriage is still considered a vulnerable and troubling figure, a man is granted a higher measure of autonomy. My husband, for instance, hasn't been receiving quite this level of solicitude. I don't think we are nearly as quick to assume that divorced men are falling into a life of despondency. I don't think that we are as concerned about what will happen to them, that we are filled with the same exquisite worry over their situation. We assume they will marry again, and until they do, we assume they're fine.

I am not trying here to make the outlandish case that I am happy. When you leave someone, there is always a small funeral going on in the back of your head. But there are also peculiar elations to this particular phase of life. It reminds me of college and shortly afterward, when you walk down the street feeling every single thing, bad and good, more vividly than you do in a more comfortable stage of life, when your feelings are more muffled. It can, of course, be hard to reconcile this overstrong feeling with the rhythms of life with a child. When I stay up until four in the morning because I have too much energy to fall asleep, because I am *thinking*, again like a college student, and then have to wake up with my daughter at six-thirty and make French toast, my body is, to say the least, perplexed.

There is something that happens when you burn your entire life down, which is the release of a strange jittery energy. The feeling is raw, close to the bone, jangly, nervous, productive. I have never, for instance, focused more on my writing or thought more clearly than in this particular time. Would I give up the book I wrote for a couple of years of happiness? Of course. But there are consolations to this kind of unhappiness; there are strange, felicitous side effects. This is one of the very few times in adult life when you get a chance to invent yourself. There is in the furious nihilism of losing someone, in the depths of how destroyed you are, a sense of terrifying openness, of absolute possibility. And if one is honest, this feeling can be perversely pleasurable.

One of the disturbing things about my marriage's breaking up, it turns out, is the feeling that I have lost a significant chunk of time to unhappiness. This may be why I don't want to give myself the "time" that people seem to think I need to recover. This may be why I don't want to wait for the ideal future when my attachments change themselves into a more conventional pattern. At a certain point, all you have are these raw, transitional hours: this is your life, and you may as well enjoy it.

I have been out at a party. I have a new dress that I have worn out to the party. The next day, I have a slightly pleasurable depleted feeling, as I push Violet in her stroller, as she eats a scone, on a twenty-minute walk to school. Later, I am out for Cobb salads on the Upper East Side with a relative who is slightly older than me. She is expressing her view that it is immature for me to be out late at parties; it is undignified for me to be floating through the night like I am in my twenties. She points out furthermore that I have a small child, a fact that I have not, in all of the hullabaloo, forgotten. Here again is the hostility toward the blurring lines, toward the falling out of categories that, I should in my defense point out, *I didn't choose.*

Recently, one of my friends ran into an acquaintance of mine at a party. She leaned into him, hand on his arm, and whispered in a confidential tone, "How's Katie?" He said, "She's great. She is having a great time teaching." This acquaintance leaned in closer, eyes widening: "How is she *really*?" My friend, a little subversive of the usual pieties, said, "I think she is the happiest woman in New York." Untrue, of course. But still, one appreciates the gesture.

One does have to wonder about the prurient hunger for unhappy detail. Is there an imperative for certain married people to believe that anyone existing outside of the institution of marriage must be suffering? Does this imperative, perhaps, have something to do with their own discontents? (The happily married couples I know are noticeably less invested in the idea that I am suffering some form of collapse. Warwick Deeping, a novelist of the twenties, observed, "Those who have made a success of marriage can be gentler to the failures.") I have noticed the couples most interested in the grand tour of my tragedy are often in couples therapy. They are often in that phase where they hire a babysitter once a week so that they can sit across from each other at a restaurant and distract themselves from the vast distance, the dullness, that has risen up between them with the bustle of menus and waiters. For whatever reason, it is extremely important for these couples to believe that once you are outside of marriage, you have fallen into the abyss. Furthermore, they are extremely interested in watching you, limbs flailing, as you are falling. But what if you, say, refuse to fall?

I begin to notice that when I am a little bit happy, there is nearly always someone there to tell me that I should be serious. That I should be focusing on my situation. That I should be worrying about my child. There is nearly always someone to deftly reel any subject I have ranged onto back to the question of whether my daughter is okay. I am, of course, always ready to worry about whether she is okay. But I wonder if it is truly in her best interest to embrace the philosophy of perpetual worry people seem to be encouraging. Wouldn't it be better to take her to the zoo?

When *The Age of Innocence* came out in 1920, the advertising leaflets began with the provocative tagline "Was She Justified in Seeking a Divorce?" And of course, this is still the question that needs to be answered. There may have been a time in the seventies when divorce was too acceptable, and even had a certain amount of cachet, but now we are back to older moral attitudes. There is still the unspoken assumption that if you worked a little bit harder, if you went to a therapist, if you tried a little harder to get along, you could have made it work, for the kids.

Someone I know almost left her husband several years ago. She had always been one of those women unusually invested in the orderliness of her life, in the outward emanations of her various perfections: her sprawling apartment on the Upper East Side, her children in their excellent schools, her scrupulously planned vacations. In thinking about her dilemma, she said, at one point, "I am not the kind of person who gets divorced! I am the kind of person who looks down on people who get divorced." This is perhaps more honest than most people would care to be on this subject.

I can't help thinking that this particular form of moral disapproval is related to our current madness about child-rearing, our desire for $900 Bugaboo strollers, Oeuf toddler beds, organic hand-milled baby food, and French classes for toddlers, not to mention sign language classes for babies so that they can communicate before they can be bothered to learn to speak: in short, our strange, hopeless obsession with the perfectibility of childhood. We seem to be laboring under the fashionable illusion that if we put all of our energy into making our children's lives ostensibly perfect, then they will be. And those of us who have separated or divorced have rather spectacularly failed in creating that perfect environment. The true stigma of divorce, at this particular moment in time, is that of failing as a parent.

On a tour of my daughter's preschool, during the question-and-answer period, one of the fathers raises his hand. He noticed a basket of pale-yellow biscuits being passed around to the four-year-olds during snack time. "What was in those cookies? Are they organic? Do they have sugar? And are the children just, um, allowed to eat as many as they want?" The headmistress of the school looks amused. No, they are not organic. Yes, they are allowed to take as many as they want. She smiles benevolently at this father. She is used to our generation's interest in controlling our children's lives. I remember the parties my parents threw, the grown-ups eating and drinking wine in the house, sometimes spilling out into the garden to smoke; the children running around outside, in bathing suits and sweatshirts, catching fireflies in jars, and no one worrying about exactly when we went to bed or whether we had four pieces of cake. Was that environment a little more forgiving of the alternative, of the house, the family that didn't look the same? I imagine it was.

In any event, the largely unspoken taboo against divorce involves the largely unspoken accusation that you are somehow behaving recklessly toward your children. But every now and then, and in different ways, someone just says it. Which is how I find myself with my most committedly bohemian, childless friend, sitting on my sofa quoting me statistics of studies that he can't quite name or define about how terrible divorce is for children. I look at him: a week of stubble, longish hair, corduroys. He has been working on a novel for the fifteen years since college; he still sleeps until four in afternoon; it would not be much of an exaggeration to say that his entire life is a monument to the refusal of adult responsibility, and yet even he is issuing grave warnings on parenting. (He is himself a child of divorce, which may account for his near-religious zeal on the subject.) I cautiously mention that in certain instances it might be better for a child if his parents don't stay in an unhappy situation. He quickly tells me that I am deluding myself, that this is a selfish platitude that parents always use to reassure themselves. He refers back to the sinister and shadowy studies. I would, again very cautiously, mention that my own child seems just for the moment to be thriving, but the evidence of the senses is not what is required here.

I have no doubt that in an ideal world, a child grows up with two happy parents under one roof. But by the time you are even contemplating divorce, you are no longer living in that ideal world and probably haven't been for a very long time. There are no true studies on the children of parents who have stayed together when they shouldn't have, no control group to tell us about the secret damage of that situation. And then, of course, there are times when the dissolution of marriage is simply unstoppable. As Theodore Dreiser put it in a 1930 essay, "God certainly has joined some peculiar creatures."

The reason this particular form of moralism is so pernicious, of course, is that it plays to your own deepest fears: you are failing at the one thing in the world that matters. To the outside eye, Violet seemed to adapt fairly quickly to the new situation. She likes when her father takes her to look at the boats on the way to school; she likes when he plays cards with her for hours at a time. But it's hard to know. She is only three. She still believes that if you drink out of someone's straw, you will become them. I can tell her elaborate bedtime stories about a group of children living on the moon. I can give her a big, warm, chaotic extended family. I can find her a tiny replica of a doctor's examination table for her eleven babies. And yet I can't give her an intact, ordinary home. Will her unorthodox childhood offer up its own consolations? One can only hope.

Last New Year's Eve, even the happiest couples around me,

who've been married for three, four, five years, seemed to be suffering a certain angst. Should they go out to a restaurant alone? Should they go to a couples' dinner party? Should they just go to a movie and pretend that it wasn't New Year's Eve? There is, of course, built into New Year's Eve, at midnight, a moment when you confront the issue of romantic intensity, the passage of time as it works on a marriage. But this year, I find myself in a slightly different world. I am walking down the street to meet a man whom I have been seeing for about a month. And while my life resembles in no outward form the way I would like it to look, the night is cold, the scraggly trees are glittering in the street lamps, the lights are on in the brownstones, and this is exactly the night I want to have.

After her own divorce, Edith Wharton wrote to one of her closest friends that she would "eat the world leaf by leaf." There are mornings when Violet pads out, in her cherry pajamas, and climbs into bed with me, and puts her face right next to mine, and I open my eyes, and her eyes are one inch away from mine, and I get out of bed and lift her up, and carry her into the kitchen, and put her on the counter, and she presses the buttons on the coffee machine, and this feels like enough. (Others will be quick to point out—others have been quick to point out—that this kind of closeness is unhealthy, that she and I are *too* connected. And to that I offer only that if you take out the unhealthy closeness, the pathological intimacies, you will have taken out many of life's wilder joys.)

One morning, Violet and I go to look at our new house, which is a construction site. There is a layer of dust over everything, the honey-colored, wide-planked floors, the white-marble fireplaces, on which one of the workers has doodled elaborately in pencil:

dragons and math problems. There are boards with nails coming out of them, paint flaking off tin ceilings, and an old, rusted refrigerator sitting in the middle of the parlor. There is a hole in the wall between the windows where a mirror has been taken down. From somewhere, our contractor has unearthed a tricycle. Before I am able to prevent it, Violet is on the tricycle, speeding through the debris. What will happen in these rooms? Violet rides over to me and is still for a minute as we look out the window at the red maple against the darkening sky.

The Alchemy of Quiet Malice

When I was pregnant with my second child, I was aware that there were many ways in which I was not prepared to take care of a baby on my own, but that awareness didn't unduly influence or affect me. What I thought to myself was "The universe will rearrange itself for this baby."

I often hear people refer to other single mothers I know as "crazy," and I assume that when I am not standing right there they refer to me that way too. I have thought about this word, especially in relation to one single mother I know who seems to me more sublimely functional and sane than anyone else I know. I began to realize that what people mean by "crazy" in this context is "romantic." They mean that she is not influenced by the practical news on the ground, is listening instead to another story that is in her head. She is drawn to things that are, according to the dictionary definition of "romantic," "impractical in conception or plan," and is in thrall to the "heroic, adventurous, remote, mysterious or idealized."

This is a common thread in the single mothers I know: they go for vividness over calm, intensity over security. One was embed-

ded with the American army in Afghanistan when she was six
months pregnant, another somehow floats with her toddler between Los Angeles, Paris, and wherever her French rail pass will
take her. Others with more pedestrian professional lives simply
decided to have a baby while their romantic lives remained complicated or turbulent or a work-in-progress. I can see why this is
"crazy" in relation to conventional, settled life, but is it crazy?
And, more important, is the term "crazy" one of our few acceptable ways of passing judgment on something different or unusual
or uncommon in a culture that is technically not supposed to be
passing those judgments?

A few months ago I came across a Pew poll showing that a
large majority of Americans still view single motherhood as unacceptable and, in the colorful words of the poll, "bad for society." Which somehow didn't surprise me. Caitlin Flanagan wrote
in *Time*, "Few things hamper a child as much as not having a father in the home." This is perhaps a little unsubtle for nice, progressive New Yorkers, and yet they think and recycle polite,
modified versions of this same idea.

To be clear, I am writing here about myself and the handful of
other single mothers I know. These are specifically women who
conceived children in some sort of relationship that they are no
longer in, and had the baby: a tiny, arguably privileged subset of
single mothers. (It is worth noting, though, that nearly four in ten
babies in this country are currently born to single mothers, and a
rapidly growing percentage of those mothers are adults. It's also
worth noting that 53 percent of babies born to women under
thirty are now born to single mothers, so it's arguably time to
stop viewing this as an exotic, or even a minority, family configu-
ration.)

Someone who was trying to persuade me not to have the baby said that I should wait and have a "regular baby." His exact words were "You could just wait and have a regular baby!" What he meant, of course, was that I should wait and have a baby in more regular circumstances. But I had seen the feet of the baby on a sonogram by this point, and while he was pacing through my living room making his point, I was thinking: This is a regular baby. His comment stayed with me, though. It evoked the word "bastard": "something that is spurious, irregular, inferior or of questionable origin."

Someone said something similar to a friend of mine when she found out that she was pregnant. He said that she should wait and have a "real baby"; and someone else referred to the children her baby's father had with his wife as his "real children." As if her baby were unreal, a figment of her imagination, as if they could wish him away.

Such small word choices, you might say. How could they possibly matter to any halfway healthy person? But it is in these choices, these casual remarks made while holding a glass of wine, these throwaway comments, these accidental bursts of honesty and flashes of discomfort, that we create a cultural climate; it's in the offhand that the judgments persist and reproduce themselves. It is here that one feels the resistance, the static, the pent-up, irrational, residual, pervasive conservatism that we do not generally own up to. Hawthorne called it "the alchemy of quiet malice, by which [we] can concoct a subtle poison from ordinary trifles."

One warm spring night my friend with the unreal baby goes to a big sprawling dinner party with children running around, at the house of some friends of friends she doesn't know very well. Toward the end of the evening the host pulls my friend aside and says that he just wanted her to know that the baby is "always welcome in our house." No one would ever say about a one-year-old with two married parents, "I just want you to know Finn is always welcome in our house." Because of course why wouldn't a one-year-old be welcome in their house? I am quite sure the man who said this sincerely felt he was being warm and hospitable and open-minded.

A novelist I know is sitting on a sunny bench in the park with his wife and two sons. He peers into the stroller at my five-pound newborn, Leo, and says, "How did *that* happen?" He smiles radiantly: It's a joke! But my six-year-old, Violet, is standing next to me, and I feel her stiffen because she senses something in his tone, something not quite nice. I say, "The usual way." But I have a feeling that if I were married he would have said something more along the lines of "congratulations."

It's around this time that I begin to see that *The Scarlet Letter* is in fact a fresh, modern commentary. One might be under the impression that tolerant liberal New York bears no resemblance to Nathaniel Hawthorne's windy Puritan New England town, but one would be wrong. Our judgments are more polite, more subtle, more psychologically nuanced and enlightened; latter-day critics of the state are thinking, of course, of what is best for the children, what is the healthiest environment; they are not opposed to extramarital philandering per se, but there is still underlying everything the same unimaginative approach to family, the same impulse to judge, the same sexual conservatism and herd mentality. The single mother traipsing up the subway steps in heels with her Maclaren is not as many worlds away as you would think from Hester Prynne.

One day one of my colleagues, noticing that I was pregnant with my second child, ducked into my office and said: "You really do whatever you want." He meant it as some variety of compliment and I took it as such, but I was beginning to get the sense that other people were looking at me and thinking the same thing; it seemed to some as if I were getting away with something, as if I were not paying the usual price, and if the usual price was take-out Thai food and a video with your husband on a Saturday night then I was not, in fact, paying that price. James Baldwin once wrote, "He can face in your life only what he can face in his own." And I imagine if you are feeling restless or thwarted in your marriage, if you have created an orderly warm home for your child at a certain slight cost to your own freedom or momentum, you might look at me, or someone else like me, and think that I am not making the usual sacrifices. (I may be making *other* sacrifices, but that is not part of this sort of calculation or judgment.)

Before I have the baby one of my friends politely suggests that it may be "hubris" to think that I can make up for the fact that the baby's father would not be in the house, and not even in the city most of the time. He tells me that I am too confident in my own powers. This worries me, sometimes late at night, because I wonder if it's not true, and there are times during the baby's first year when I wish the earth would stop spinning so that I can get off for a moment and rest. But it also occurs to me that this may be the good and useful kind of hubris.

The submerged premise here is that there is something greedy, selfish, narcissistic, or antisocial about having a baby on your own. But is there? It seems to me that if anything a baby born in these conditions is extra-wanted. The fact that having that baby is not necessarily the obvious or normal or predictable or easy thing to do at this particular juncture in life makes it all the more of a deep and consuming commitment.

At lunch I mention to an editor that I am thinking of writing about single mothers and the subtle and not-so-subtle forms our moralism toward them takes. He says, "That's a good idea. And I say that as a guy who looks at single women and thinks what's wrong with her? How did she fuck up?"

It's spring and I am invited to give a talk out of town. I am on the phone with a friend who is a psychiatrist, and I ask if she thinks the baby will be okay if I leave him for a night. He is one and a half, and I have never left him for a whole night. I should mention that I am not here thinking of leaving him in a nightclub. I am thinking of leaving him with the babysitter who has been with us for eight years, and has been taking care of him his whole life. "Do you think he'll be all right?" "Probably," she says. "Of course, it would be better if you had a husband in the house." I say that I may not be able to get one by Wednesday.

My friend Sonya, a very beautiful Indian woman who works in fashion, had her daughter on her own when she was twenty-eight. She got married a year later to another man, and then left him, and is now on her own with her daughter. She says it's almost worse when hostile or complicated comments come from her liberal neighbors in Brooklyn: "Who are they to tell me I'm hindered or handicapped in some way? They are all invested in keeping up appearances. Some of them are like, I've sucked up my crappy marriage, why haven't you sucked up your crappy marriage? And then there is a kind of strange fascination. Like someone I barely know will ask me if my daughter's dad pays child support. And I am like, Is that any of your business? Do I ask you if you paid your taxes last year?" I know what she means. When you are pregnant, strangers feel like they can come up to you and touch you; when you are a single mother, strangers feel like they can come up to you and ask you anything. It is as if you have somehow given people who barely know you permission to say something intimate or invasive simply by having a baby without a man in the house.

Sonya remembers a single mother friend of hers warning her not to wear a certain dress to a garden party full of couples, but she puts it on anyway, and digs out a pair of stilettos. When she walks into the party, there are a bunch of women clumped around the bar in the kitchen, and hardly any of them will talk to her or look at her, and later she leaves feeling as if she has spent the last four hours sitting in a traffic jam or waiting in a doctor's office, instead of going to a party. Should she not have worn the dress? "I am at the point where I am not going to apologize for myself," she says. "But it's exhausting. It takes a lot of energy."

In spite of our exquisite tolerance for all kinds of lifestyles, we have a wildly outdated but strangely pervasive idea that single motherhood is worse for children, somehow a compromise, a flawed venture, a grave psychological blow to be overcome, our enlightened modern version of shame. It malingers, this idea; it affects us still.

The power of this view is that it very easily gets inside your head, it resonates with every children's book you have ever read about little bear families, with all the archaic visions of family that cohere in the furthest reaches of your imagination: It's hard to free yourself. It's hard not to interrogate your own choices, hard not to offer up elaborate excuses or explanations.

I notice the tendency in myself is toward jokes, toward a kind of hard, protective mockery. I find that I am very deliberately not apologizing for the baby by embracing the most ridiculous, tabloidy words for him, like "love child." I hear myself spinning a caricature of my semi-bohemian household when I run into someone at a party I haven't seen in a while: "Yeah, two babies, two different dads. I somehow ended up with the family structure Pat Moynihan was complaining about."

In fact, by now I have spent so long outside of conventional family life that sometimes when I spend an afternoon with married friends and their children, their way of life seems exotic to me. The best way I can describe this is the feeling of being in a foreign country where you notice the bread is good and the coffee excellent but you are not exactly thinking of giving it all up and living there.

In the weeks after the baby was born my sense of family was burned down and clarified. I began to see that some of the people related to me by blood were not my family, and some of my friends and ex-flames were. In some way the definition became very basic and pared down, like the person you can call to drive you to the hospital in the middle of the night is your family. My family was suddenly voluntary, elective, chosen: a great thing I came to late.

The baby refers to his sister's father, Harry, as "My Harry," as in "My Harry is coming!" It seems to me the exuberant, unorthodox use of pronoun gets at the conjuring, the act of creation, the interesting magic trick at the center of the whole venture: his family will be what he makes it.

Leo is two, but he chooses his own people. He picks fatherish figures, including his own father. I notice people often find little ways of telling me that *it's not the same thing*. And of course it's not, but it seems a bit narrow-minded or overly literal to think that love has to come from two parents, like water from hot and cold faucets.

But is it more stable or secure to grow up in a house with two parents? There is arguably an absence of what people like to call borders in my house. For instance the baby seems to have caught my insomnia. Before going to bed he howls like a wolf, then says, "I am a wolf," then says, "Where is my bottle? Where is my mango? Where is my ketchup?" then very deliberately climbs out of his bed and walks through the dark halls saying, "I am lost, Mama, I am lost." It occurs to me that in this unfiltered, unmediated environment I am passing everything along to him. In any event, that's exactly how I feel at two in the morning—somewhere smack dab in the middle of "I am lost" and "Where is my mango? Where is my ketchup?"

I am quite prepared to believe that in a household with two adults, there is generally a little more balance, a healthy dilution of affection, a diffused focus that makes everyone feel comfortable. One morning I overhear Violet saying to the baby, "You can't marry anyone. You are going to live with me." When I first separated from her father, she said, at three, "Mommy, it's like you and *I* are married." And this would pretty accurately reflect the atmospherics of our house: a little too much love, you might tactfully say.

Quentin Bell once wrote about growing up with his single-ish mother, the painter Vanessa Bell: "We had to balance the comforts of being so well loved against the pain of being so fearfully adored." And that seems like a fair assessment of what goes on in my house and those of other single mothers I know. (The grown son of one of them refers to this as "the unparalleled intimacy.") But if I am being honest, I like the fearful adoration, the too-muchness of it, the intensity, the fierceness. I don't actually believe "healthy" is better.

I also can't help noticing that the people talking about a "healthy" environment are often the same people talking about "working" on their relationships. They are often the denizens of couples therapy and date nights in restaurants that serve hand-cured pancetta and organic local fennel; I have no doubt that they do create a healthy, balanced environment, but I like to think there are some rogue advantages to the unbalanced and unhealthy environment, to the other way of doing things.

Here someone is bound to say, "Studies have shown . . ." And as far as I am concerned the studies can continue to show whatever they feel like showing. There are things that can't be measured and quantified in studies, and I imagine the multitudinous varieties of family peace are among them. Not to mention what these stern and admonitory studies fail to measure, which is what happens when there is anger or conflict in the home, or unhappy or airless marriages, relationships wilting or faltering, subterranean tensions, what happens when everyone is bored.

One also has to take into account that the realities of American family life no longer match its prevailing fantasies. One of the reasons children born outside of marriage suffer is the culturally ubiquitous idea that there is something wrong or abnormal about their situation. Once it becomes clear that there is, at least, nothing abnormal about their situation—i.e., when the 53 percent of babies born to women under thirty come of age in the majority—the psychological landscape, at least, will be vastly transformed.

Even people who are certain that the children of single mothers are always and forever doomed to a compromised existence are going to have to await more information about a world in which these kids are not considered illegitimate or unconventional or outsiders, where the sheer number of them redefines and refreshes our ideas of family.

There is no doubt that raising a child on your own is different than raising a child with a partner, it's apples and oranges, but what progressive American culture is not currently prepared to acknowledge is that there are advantages to each. My friend Cristina Nehring, who is also a single mother, writes in an email from Paris that she has observed that kids in single-parent households "are often rendered more mature, caring and empathic. Kids in two-parent households risk viewing their parents as an amorphous unit of authority, as a kind of faceless ruling elite, a wall of adult power. This can be useful for crude discipline in the short term, but it's less useful in terms of the development of empathy and imagination in the long term. Kids of mono-parental families have more and earlier opportunities than their peers to recognize that adults have stories and sensitivities and struggles of their own. In today's age of imperious, entitled super-children, the kids of single parents often grow up a bit more modest and humane."

It's fascinating to me that she would say this because of course part of what people think children miss in a single mother's home is the steadiness and security of that "amorphous unit of authority." Part of what seems threatening or unsettling about the single mother's household is precisely that sense that the mother may be glimpsed as more of a person, that these children are witnessing a struggle they should not be seeing, that their mother is very early on a regular, complicated person, rather than simply an adult who is part of the opaque, semi-separate adult culture of the house.

One day at dinner, Violet is playing a game where she is listing impossible things. Like it's impossible to talk when you are dead, or it's impossible for a human to fly without a machine, when she suddenly comes out with "It's impossible to be normal." The family member in attendance shoots me a look that eloquently points out that Violet might not think it was so impossible to be normal if instead of piles of books on the floor I had a little financial security, if I had a man around the house. If I stopped running around like I do, in other words.

It's near dawn when I finish *The Scarlet Letter* and I had forgotten the ending. Hawthorne is careful to tell us that Pearl, wild, untamed, radiant, spritelike Pearl, grows up and leaves for Europe, where she is happy and flourishing; the suggestion is that she is perhaps a bit happier than the children of the drab Puritan town she has left behind.

It's getting dark and I am stepping into a taxi, the parlor window is lit, the children at home in their pajamas, smelling of Johnson & Johnson's, domestic peace descending, and I go off in a car to meet a man at a hotel bar. This will seem like the wrong structure to many people; they will tell me how unhealthy it is, how unsustainable, how unstable, and they may be right, but there I am speeding across the bridge nonetheless. There are other possible ways I could conduct my life, other forms and structures. But I remember hearing somewhere: "You have one life, if that." And one sometimes feels like mentioning that to some of the more blinkered respectable couples, to those purveyors of wholesome and healthy environments, to those who truly believe the child of a single mother is not whole or happy in his room playing with his dinosaurs: You have one life, if that.

Unquiet Americans

1

I spent more time than was strictly necessary in the plush red corridors of the Hotel Metropole in Hanoi. For some reason, I had convinced myself that I needed to see the inside of suite 228, which was otherwise referred to in the voluminous hotel literature as "the Graham Greene Suite." Greene, whom I had been mildly fixated on for some time, had stayed there during the fifties. I was staying next door in suite 226, and after several days of wondering how I was going to get into his room, I noticed the maid's cart outside. When she finally ducked out to refill her stash of aloe shampoo and little almond soaps, I slipped through the half-opened door. Inside was a bare mahogany desk, a brass lamp, a king-size bed with a modern, striped duvet, and several spindly French sofas, also striped. I couldn't help feeling vastly let down. The setting was devoid of both Greene's seediness— he later regretted popularizing the word "seedy"—and his elegance, which should not, of course, have come as a surprise. The

Metropole was gutted after the war and rebuilt. And even if it hadn't been, I knew from experience that this sort of literary pilgrimage is always anticlimactic: the writer is dead and what remains of him is in his books.

Luckily in Greene's case the books are everywhere. It's almost impossible to walk down the street in Hanoi without stumbling across a sky-blue Penguin edition of *The Quiet American*. If one looks closely enough, the black-and-white photograph of a gun emerging from long grasses on the cover is slightly blurred, and if one flips through the pages the words themselves are also blurred, which is because they are pirated copies, photocopied from the originals. When I first spotted the cheerful, familiar blue covers, I was taken aback, as if my private relation to the book were cheapened; it somehow bothered me to see Greene's morally complicated vision hawked to tourists, but then everything was hawked to tourists, and wasn't I, when it came down to it, a tourist myself? In a way, its commercial ubiquity is something the book could have predicted of itself. The novel foretells a Vietnam in the thrall of what it calls "dollar love," and Westerners in thrall right back.

By the time we reached Hanoi, my then husband and I had been traveling through Asia for almost a month. I had begun to see that everywhere we went there were a million minor transactions taking place beneath the surface. At first I was oblivious to these transactions, but slowly I began to recognize them: if a driver takes you to his friend's hotel, he is getting a cut; if a waiter sells you an expensive dish, he is getting a cut; if a guide takes you to a silk shop, he is getting a cut; and there are bound to be other people getting cuts of his cut. If you watch these transactions closely enough, you begin to get the feeling of an ant farm, a honeycomb, thousands of tiny gestures replicating themselves.

On one of our first days in Bangkok we made our way to the Grand Palace. We could see the gold roof of the main pagoda glinting behind a wall. A man pointed us down a street to the entrance. It seemed a long way, so we asked again and two other men pointed us in the same direction. When we got to the end of the street, a cyclo driver told us that the Grand Palace was closed, and he would take us to another temple and then back for a dollar. An old man came over to translate his offer. In fact, the Grand Palace was not closed. The entrance was in the other direction. This scheme employed five men for an afternoon.

After a while, we began to get used to the idea that for small amounts of money, the facts were willing to alter themselves. At a jumbled antiques store across from the Metropole, we picked up a coy-looking stone Buddha with its hands on its hips. "It is from the seventeenth century," the woman with serious glasses behind the counter informed us. When we returned later that afternoon, it was from the nineteenth century.

We bought it, whatever it was, and went out for a late lunch. I looked over at my husband dipping a dumpling in sauce, and I noticed that he had been physically transformed. He is one of the few people I know who looks most himself in a suit and tie. In his closet at home, he keeps wooden shoe trees in his shoes, which he polishes himself in a ritual that takes over our entire living room for an afternoon. But as soon as we arrived, he stopped shaving. He started wearing sandals that Velcroed across the toes. At some point, without my realizing it, his appearance had passed beyond scruffy into the netherworld of international drifters who float through Asia staying in guest houses without clean sheets. I am not sure whether this was a subliminal attempt at disguise, but if it was, it didn't work.

One staggeringly hot day, we took a motorcycle through the rice paddies to a nearby beach and stopped at a stretch of creamy sand with mountains rising from the ocean. But as soon as we took off our shoes, dozens of children clustered around us trying to get us to sit under their umbrellas.

When we finally laid out our towels and settled down with our books, two sturdy-looking girls came to offer pedicures and necklaces. "My name Hong Kong," one of them said. They crouched next to us. They showed no signs of moving. The one that was not Hong Kong sulked theatrically. "Bad day. No one buy Buddhas." She fanned out the jade necklaces she was selling.

"I don't have any money," I told her.

"He has money," said Hong Kong, gesturing toward my husband.

"He doesn't want to buy anything."

"He change mind."

"I never change my mind," he said.

"You change mind."

"Madam, you want? Tell him you want, he change mind."

"But I don't want one."

The green Buddhas glittered in the sand.

"If we stay he change mind."

"I never change my mind," he said again.

They squatted near our feet. One of them rested her head on my arm. We tried to look out at the ocean.

"You need souvenir? You remember day?"

They sat with us for an hour, resuming their sales pitch every now and then. "You buy one?" "You buy two?" They were harassing us, but sweetly. Their presence changed the nature of the activity. We were not sitting on the beach the way we think of sitting on the beach at home.

"You change mind?" They went over to my husband. Hong Kong put her hands on her hips and studied him.

"No."

The shadow of a cloud moved across the sand. Suddenly I needed a souvenir to remember the day.

"Let's just get one," I said. We bought a jade Buddha on a strip of leather.

"He change mind!" they said triumphantly. "He change mind!" We gave them a dollar. Interestingly, it was my husband who put the Buddha around his neck.

We paid in dollar bills because street sellers prefer them here. In other countries one pays for familiar-looking items with brightly colored bills that look and feel like Monopoly money. But here it is the opposite: every element of life is different, the air, the sun, the dense, sweet coffee, the dragon fruit we eat for breakfast with its curling fuchsia rind like lapping tongues, the lizards that dapple the walls of elegant restaurants like patterned wallpaper. The only thing that is familiar, the only thing that moors us to our regular lives, is the green face of our former president.

2

In Phnom Penh, the proprietors of our hotel have placed a dis-
creet gold plaque on the reception desk that reads NO CHILD SEX
TOURISM. If this warning is regarded at all, it is regarded quite
literally, because outside on a chaise longue near the pool lies a
sullen-looking Khmer girl in a leopard-print bikini who looks
no older than fourteen. The German next to her has graying,
wiry hair, tortoiseshell glasses, and a perfectly round, pregnant-
looking stomach emerging from his Speedo bathing suit. He is
talking avidly into his cellphone. After a little while they go into
the pool. She lies on her back and closes her eyes. He holds her up
as if she were a child learning to float.

They flock here, men too lonely, too fat, too ugly, too lazy, to
pick up a woman in their local bar in Marseille, Duluth, or Baden-
Baden. They seem to find it reassuring that the line between pros-
titution and normal life is blurred; that a man can go to a bar and
pick up a beautiful woman who will be his girlfriend if he buys
her things, and who will continue to be his girlfriend if he continues to buy her things.

One night in Bangkok at a pretty outdoor restaurant on the
canal, we are seated next to a little dumpling of a man with pale
blue crinkling eyes. He is wearing a crisply ironed white shirt and
a black suit and his face is overwhelmed by an enormous black
cowboy hat.

"You like shrimp?" he says in heavily accented English.

"Very much," murmurs the Thai woman across from him.

"You are very pretty."

The evening smells of smog and burning leaves. The lights of the restaurant flicker in the black water.

"More champagne?"

"Thank you."

The eye is drawn to the improbably wide brim of the cowboy hat with its braided tassel and turquoise tips. The man flags down the waitress for another bottle of champagne. It's clear that he is going all out. No romantic flourish will be spared. He is determined to be a man enjoying a romantic evening instead of a man paying for a woman, determined to experience seduction, even in a situation where seduction is ludicrous. This, it occurs to me, is where one can find Graham Greene. Here in the relationships between Western men and the Eastern women whose company they are purchasing or half purchasing. Whenever Greene describes the allure of the East, women are always intricately involved: he wrote, "The spell was first cast by the tall elegant girls in white silk trousers, by the pewter evening light on flat paddy fields." And in *The Quiet American*, his British and American characters cannot help developing dangerous romantic fantasies, and his Vietnamese heroine remains cool, untouched.

Greene himself was attracted to both the idea and the reality of prostitutes and taxi girls. When he was in Saigon he frequented the House of Four Hundred Women on the rue de Catinat, which he fictionalizes in *The Quiet American* as the House of Five Hundred Women. In fact his view of ordinary romantic relationships was so bleak that it is easy to see how the simplicity of a purchased evening would appeal. For him, love affairs caused endless amounts of savagery and bitterness, and watching love fade, he observed over and over, was like death itself. Marriage, it goes without saying, was even worse; he wrote coolly, "There is nothing so charmless as the company of a woman who is no longer desired." And in the end, what is interesting about Greene is the strain of desperate emotional blackness. Beneath the surface of his bestselling adventure stories was a sensibility so bruised that prostitutes seemed purer than the demanding women from home. In one of my favorite photographs of him, Greene, in a cable-knit Irish sweater, is stretched out lankily on a beach blanket with his great love, Catherine Walston. But even with her he is irrita-ble and gloomy. He could never rid himself of his obsession with the transactions beneath relationships, the transactions that we keep hidden in the West, the transactions that surface so easily here.

A few weeks later, we find ourselves in a café in Hanoi that serves lattes and cappuccinos to Westerners who have grown tired of thick, sweet Vietnamese coffee with condensed milk.

I hear a man's voice saying, "When we get home you shower with me—I will wash your back."

The voice is coming from a chunky American in his fifties with a long mustache and a plaid button-down shirt, short sleeves rolled up to reveal an elaborately fanged dragon tattoo. He is sit-ting across from a young, not quite pretty Vietnamese woman.

"Lots of the girls there want to be my girlfriend. There is one girl, I spend many nights with her. She wants to be my girlfriend."

I can't hear how the woman responds because she speaks too softly.

"Shouldn't your sister be helping to pay for your father?"

She murmurs something unintelligible.

He says, "I will send you two, maybe three million dong."

The waiter swoops down to clear their plates. The man places a ten-dollar bill on the table. "You're staring," my husband points out. I have the terrible habit of turning to stare at the people I am eavesdropping on. I try to turn my attention back to my croque monsieur.

We watch countless scenes like this everywhere we go. At first, I feel a twinge of superiority, but over time this superiority dissipates. And in the end the trip is quite humbling. It reminds me of one of the ancient temples at Angkor Wat, which is made up of a series of concentric walls, each one ringed around another. The doorways carved into the stone are made progressively lower as you move toward the shrine at the center. The architecture physically forces you to bow.

3

From the moment I stepped onto the boat on Cambodia's vast Tonle Sap lake I had a premonition that something bad was going to happen. For one thing, it lacked seriousness. It looked like the kind of brightly painted wooden boat that children play with in fountains. Emerging from the dashboard was an unpromising collection of wires in various states of unravelment held together by duct tape, and the usual accoutrements of safety, such as radios or life preservers, were notably missing. The windows were so small that if the boat tipped over, as it was known to do from time to time, we would all be trapped inside and drowned. And the captain had sold so many tickets that half of the passengers had to sit cross-legged on the flat roof. Sixty people were crammed with luggage into a boat made for twenty-five. Greene wrote that what attracted him to this part of the world was "the exhilaration which a measure of danger brings to a visitor with a return ticket," but I didn't feel anything like that exhilaration. When the engines started and the nose of the boat began to bounce on the choppy water, and everyone else started clapping and cheering, it seemed to me that we were casually ferrying to our deaths.

After an hour or so, we were in the middle of the giant, milky brown lake. The trees were a distant fringe around the shore. And suddenly an alarm sounded, a mournful electrical cry from the depths of the water. It meant, though none of us knew at the time, that we had run aground. The reason none of us knew it at the time was that the crew spoke no English. The passengers, with the exception of one Chinese-speaking man, spoke no Khmer.

The boat sat motionless. There was nothing we could do but wait. The heat was astonishing; temperatures had been hovering around 120 degrees and the low roof of the cabin seemed to press in on us. Some of the passengers began sticking their heads out of the tiny windows to get air. Others became annoyed that they were getting less air because of the people who were plugging the windows with their heads. One man, a French chef vacationing with his parents, had a cooler abundantly packed with beer, ice cubes, and pâté sandwiches on French bread. The rest of us eyed him suspiciously. On the way to the dock, my husband and I had picked up a dust-coated bottle of water from one of the floating villages, but I noticed we only had a few sips left. I thought about our bodies swelling on the glassy brown surface of the lake, the parching of our throats, the slow blackening of our skin; my husband leafed through the *Herald Tribune*.

Eventually I climbed up on top of the boat where the younger passengers were already roasting and pinkening in the sun. An American college student was trying to get a signal on the international cellphone his parents had given him in case of emergencies; a British woman with a kerchief around her head had taken out a water filter that she claimed would clean the typhoid and bacteria from the murky lake water. Narrow sampans glided by, little children squatting in the bows. They looked up at us with wide eyes: fat pink foreigners stuffed into an unmoving boat.

At this point the sun was still swollen and high in the sky, but in a few hours it would be dark. Even if we somehow made it to shore, the surrounding jungle was not necessarily safer than the middle of the lake. There were not necessarily roads with cars. The jungle floor was laced with land mines. The day before we left, we had stopped to listen to a band made up entirely of musicians with various limbs blown off.

The American student mentioned the possibility of the embassy sending a helicopter to lift us to safety. The British couple chuckled. The Australians exchanged glances. Here was an American attitude of the type Greene satirized so elegantly in *The Quiet American*. And of course, he was right. The assumptions about movement that we generally take for granted, namely, that there will be someone we can pay to take us to where we want to go, suddenly seemed naïve and oddly irrelevant.

If only we had flown. We had thought of flying. Most tourists, with the exception of grubby backpackers and committed bohemians, fly from Siem Reap to Phnom Penh. From the sky you can see how astonishing the landscape is: Rivers the color of chocolate milk running through grassy fields. Sugar palms sticking up from the flat earth. The rich green and gold brush of rice paddies divided neatly into squares. But then, in Cambodia even flying involves all of the country's eccentricities: according to the local papers, a plane was recently delayed for hours by a stray dog wandering onto a landing strip.

I climbed back into the cabin because I could feel my face getting burned. I took my old seat next to my husband, who was still immersed in the *Herald Tribune*. In fact his nonchalance was beginning to attract attention. The round, merry Malaysian man on my other side started calling him "Moon Man" and "Man from the Moon," since he was the only person on board who did not seem to be alarmed by our situation, this when he wasn't congratulating me on having such a tall husband.

Six hours later, a rickety wooden boat with a motor tied to it with string sputtered up next to our ferry. Half of us got off and stood on the boat in the sun. There wasn't room to sit. Water pooled at our ankles, seeping in through the gaps in the wood. The makeshift boat tugged the other boat, slowly, to deeper waters. We could see the angled silhouettes of pagodas and palm leaves against the flame-colored sky. Eleven and a half hours after we set out, we arrived in Phnom Penh.

As we stood on the dock in the gathering dusk, I felt shaken. One of the shirtless crew members standing on top of the boat with a cigarette dangling from his lips tossed my luggage to my feet. I tried to smile at him but he didn't smile back. And I saw that what had distressed and slightly shocked me about the boat ride was the hostility, the contempt of the crew. When a group of passengers went up to try to talk to the captain, he waved them away like an emperor dismissing the girls coming to fan him with banana leaves. In fact the crew was finding it amusing, if anything, to watch white faces turning various shades of fuchsia in the beating sun. They sat on the roof and smoked. They plumped up our luggage like pillows and sprawled across it, joking with each other in Khmer. When the resourceful British woman with the water filter tried to ask them if someone was coming to help us, they imitated her question in a shrill, mocking tone: "Excuse me, is a boat coming to help us?" Normally, when there is not a crisis, one doesn't feel this kind of hostility; the language barrier is strong enough, the moving boat itself enough distraction, but there, stuck in the middle of the lake, in the stillness, the brilliant green of the jungle melting into the sky, it was impossible not to see. Of course, we had been experiencing this hostility, this mocking, all along: in the faces of the children hawking post-cards, in the sinewy necks of the cyclo drivers who pedaled our heavy foreign bodies up hills. Of course, it's always there in a tourist culture—when the people are poor and the tourists are rich, the power smolders and turns very easily into something ugly. It is the modern version of the rage against colonials in *A Passage to India* or *The Jewel in the Crown*. It is the contempt of the seller for those who are sold to.

4

During our eleven and a half hours on the boat, I conceived a desire to stay at the Royal Hotel in Phnom Penh. The Royal is more expensive than any of the hotels that we encountered on the trip, and we had encountered expensive hotels. In a city renowned for its lawlessness, a city where guidebooks warn that armed theft happens regularly—rumors abound that it may be the local police doing the robberies—a city where the streets are still un-walkable at night, the rates are nothing short of astonishing. But this, of course, is part of the point. I picture a lobby with soaring ceilings, sweeping staircases, milk-white columns and marble floors; rooms with mahogany four-poster beds, burnished Buddha heads with tight gold curls, plates of croissants, fluffy bathrobes, and slippers with little insignia on them. I am feeling unsafe.

Even under normal circumstances, I find grand old colonial hotels infinitely comforting: the rattan chairs, the potted palms, the ceiling fans, the general ambience of gin and tonics about to arrive with a slice of lime. These hotels tend to overdo themselves, like movie sets, but the overdoing itself is what makes them comforting. The bars have names like Elephant Bar. The gift shops have glass cases, where rings and necklaces nestle in velvet cushions. The doors are manned by turbaned doormen. Outside a man prods you with his stump and smiles; the air smells of incense and rotting fruit; the sound of motorcycles pierces the night like gunfire. But the bombardment of the street is somehow framed and miniaturized by a hotel like this; it is put in perspective; it is the culture that you have flown all this way to observe, manageable as a postcard.

"Let's stay at the Royal Hotel," I say when we slip into the taxi. I say this knowing that my husband prefers another sort of hotel. His taste runs toward the ramshackle, the family-run. He prefers inns like the tiny three-hundred-year-old house in Hoi An where we rented a room with intricately carved mahogany walls and ceilings, and a red velvet bed draped in frothy mosquito netting. He finds the theatrical colonialism of places like the Royal off-putting, and, of course, he's right to, but I am undeterred in my desire for the wrong sort of hotel. I am thinking about a room without lizards climbing the wall.

"The Royal Hotel?" He raises his eyebrows. "Expensive taste for a housewife."

I look out the window. I am filled with rage. I am coated in a layer of dirt from the boat. My luggage is coated in a layer of dirt from the boat. Could I have misheard? Is he actually saying that I can't choose our hotel because I am a housewife? It is true that I have spent the last year musing on my next book, reading and plotting and taking notes, and he has largely been supporting me. I hadn't thought of it so starkly, but when it comes down to it he is paying for the trip. The money for the hotel room is his, I realize; he should decide where we stay. I am suddenly over-whelmed by my own helplessness. How have I allowed myself to slip into this maddening, 1950s-style dependence? Why hadn't I noticed it before? A line from *The Quiet American* comes to mind: "The hurt is in the act of possession: we are too small in mind and body to possess another person without pride, or to be possessed without humiliation."

The car weaves through throngs of motorcycles, some of which are piled high with entire families, and stops at a red light. Outside the city menaces. The dusty, saffron-colored buildings have crumbling walls and peeling wooden shutters and wrought-iron terraces spilling over with bougainvillea. Everything looks charming and decrepit and chipped. It looks like Paris, if Paris had sunk to the bottom of the sea for decades.

"What's wrong?" my husband asks.

I look out the window.

"We can stay there if you want. I was just kidding."

In fact, he was only referring to my filling in the occupation "housewife" on my visa application so as to avoid the complications that would arise from filling in "writer" or "journalist." He was not calling me a housewife, though for a moment our relation to each other feels jittery.

The truth is that this exchange would never have happened anywhere else. It involves a way of thinking that is alien to both of us. What is mine. What is his. The misunderstanding surfaces here because of the perpetual marketplace; because female company is so easily, so ubiquitously, for sale.

5

Our guide in Cambodia is tiny and immaculate, his plaid button-down shirt tucked into black khakis, a belt around his waist. He is so nervous and self-effacing that we pick him out of the crowd of touts who have been waiting on the dock for eleven and a half hours for our boat to arrive. They are all waving signs and shouting, "Taxi! Hotel! Taxi! Hotel!" But our guide seems embarrassed by the idea of having to sell his services. He is wincing with embarrassment. He has the floppy hair of an English schoolboy, and his voice is so soft that we have to lean in close to him to make out what he is saying.

Early the next morning, he takes us to the abandoned high school, once known as Security Prison 21, where the Khmer Rouge tortured and killed thousands of their own people. It is a low, undistinguished-looking cement structure built around a courtyard and surrounded with barbed wire. There are people milling around with cameras around their necks. But it is not a museum the way we have museums; it is not polished the way we expect museums to be polished. There are bloodstains on the stone floors, for instance. There are rusting bed frames where prisoners were tortured. There are wooden bars that they were chained to lying down. There is not enough light. Our guide leads us quickly from one room to the next. He goes out of his way to touch everything with his hands. As we make our way through the courtyard, it feels more like a crime scene that has been blocked off with yellow tape than a museum. The tragedy feels fresh, the air disturbed.

Afterward our guide drives us to the Killing Fields. Within blocks the stone edifices of the city dissolve into palm-thatched huts on stilts. The pavement gives way to a rough dirt road embedded with stones. Our driver's silver Timex looks bulky on his fragile wrist as he steers around the larger rocks and holes. It is impossible to tell how old he is—he could be twenty or forty-five. People here tend to look very, very young until all of a sudden they look very, very old. As the car bounces along, we manage to look out the window at the jackfruit trees. I have never seen jackfruits before. They are green and bumpy and scrunched up: they look like women's handbags hanging from trees.

The ride takes longer than we expected. We hadn't really wanted to go to the Killing Fields in the first place. We anticipated the eerie lushness, the indifferent, picnic-ground green common to sites of mass murder. But our guide, in his gentle, unassuming way, was adamant.

When we finally arrive, as we had suspected, there is not much to see. There are ditches and delicate, drooping trees. There are several clusters of tourists murmuring in cemetery tones. Our guide calls me "Lady," as he directs me to the best view: "Lady, you stand here."

He tells us that the Khmer Rouge killed babies by swinging them against a tree. He mimes the gesture and says, "They like for mothers to see."

At the end of our tour, our guide brings us over to a blossoming frangipani tree and says softly, "Now I will tell you about my family." The fragrance of the white blossoms fills the air. We lean in closer to hear him. With the wind it is almost impossible to make out what he is saying. It occurs to me that as we were jostled on the dock, with all of the touts trying to shepherd us toward their taxis, our guide had said, "I will tell you about my family's experiences."

Our guide tells us that planes circled his village on the border of Vietnam, spraying white napalm onto the thatched roofs. His three-year-old brother and four-year-old sister died of burns as the family fled with all of their belongings through the jungle.

He speaks quietly and without expression in his far-from-perfect English. He mimes the situations he can't find words for, holding his arms around his stomach to communicate that his other sister was pregnant when she stepped on a land mine, years later, at around the same time that his uncle and cousins were abducted by the Khmer Rouge. "It is still difficult here," he concludes. "I have to pay money to send my children to school." He leads us past a monument of skulls piled high in a glass case. Three Cambodian schoolgirls are chatting up a group of Japanese men, their giggles rising to the trees. And as we walk back to the car, I have the feeling we have just paid for something you are not supposed to pay for.

A few days later, we fly home. As soon as we unpack, the trip recedes into a series of benign and picturesque images: the pink dawn against the pineapple towers of Angkor Wat, the tall, elegant girls in white silk trousers, the pewter evening light on flat paddy fields. But there on our mantel is the chipped stone Buddha from the seventeenth or nineteenth or twenty-first century; the shifting, bought object, plundered, beautiful, faked; it stands there, smiling, in our house.

Beautiful Boy, Warm Night

My memory of Stella, at nineteen, is neither as crisp nor as detailed as it should be. It's only with a tremendous effort of will that I can bring her into focus at all. She is wearing a complicated black outfit that looks like rags pinned together with safety pins, and black stockings, with deliberate runs laddering her legs. Her skin is translucent, the color of skim milk, and her matted, dyed blond hair looks about as plausibly human as the hair of a much-loved doll. Under her eyes are extravagant circles, plum-colored and deep. She always looks haggard. No one that age looks haggard the way she looked haggard, and yet as one came to know her, that was part of her romance.

Stella was from the South. I remember her being from a trailer park, but it may have been a small town. She had some sort of unspeakable tragedy in her background, which added to the quality of Southern gothic she cultivated. In my picture of her, she is curled up on a mahogany windowsill with a Faulkner novel, but in reality, she was one of those brilliant college students whose minds are clamoring too loudly with their own noise to read much.

On good days, Stella looked as if she were late to the most important meeting of her life; on bad days, she looked if she were being hunted down by organized and insidious forces. She was also one of the most powerful people in our Harvard class. She was monumentally, conspicuously damaged in a way that was, to us then, ineffably chic. She had an entourage of followers and hangers-on, mostly men of ambiguous sexual preference whose mothers had given them exotic, weighty names like Byron and Ulysses. She had an authentically doomed streak that was to the rest of us, future bankers, editors, and lawyers, future parents and mortgage holders, uniquely appealing. And the whole time I knew her she was writing something—a detective story? a play? a thriller?—something with a murder in it, I think, but whatever it was, it added to the impression that she was engaged in more important endeavors than the rest of us. She talked in the cartoon bubbles of comic-book characters: "Oh-ho." Or "Jumping Juniper." Or "Iced cold beverage," or "Eek." This was part of an elaborate, stylized defense, against the softness associated with sincerity.

And yet, the perfection of her cool was pleasantly undermined by an ambience of frazzled vulnerability. She was overweight, and had a flinching relationship with her own body. If you caught a glimpse of her coming down Plympton Street at dusk, you might mistake her self-deprecating shuffle for that of a homeless person. In retrospect, I can see that she was kind of wonderful-looking, with her fabulous, disheveled gestalt, but at the time being overweight was an enormous, almost insurmountable, taboo. She had a great, pure throaty laugh, which went along with a child's pleasure in the smallest things. I can see her face lighting up over a chocolate sundae or a gardenia-scented candle.

She was one of the few girls at school that I could talk to. We would sit on her bed and chatter for hours. She would smoke insane numbers of cigarettes. I would drink insane amounts of coffee. In the background a scratchy Lou Reed song called "Street Hassle" might be playing, a song that for some reason we couldn't get enough of. It was about a party interrupted by the inconvenient discovery of a girl who has died of an overdose.

Over the years the sting of what happened between us has died down to an anecdote repeated at cocktail parties, where I had found it could be interesting sometimes to reveal something odious about yourself. "Will you listen to how you sound?" I can hear Stella saying. "It's still all about what a colorful character *you* are, isn't it?" In my mind her voice is perpetually and sharply sarcastic, which it wasn't always. There was plenty to Stella besides her considerable satiric gifts. But that is, after all of these years, what remains.

Stella's one conventionality was that she was in love. The boy in question was very tall and very green-eyed. He wore ripped jeans and fake gas station attendant's shirts, and was a Buddhist. He had a funny, fluid way of moving his long arms and legs that was attractively effeminate and moderately vain. And he had elegant, sharply arched eyebrows that gave him the aspect of one of the wickeder Greek gods. I won't bother to say what his name was because he could have been anyone, and his specific personality, which was fairly annoying in a number of specific ways, would only be a sideshow and a distraction. I knew the night I met him and Stella that they both were and weren't together;

both facts were equally apparent after being around either of them for five minutes. They orbited each other, but anxiously. They spoke the same weird patois, a mixture of baby talk and archness. ("Who was that female person you were talking to?" "I don't know to whom you are referring, doll.") They seemed, if anything, like a brother and sister engaged in some kind of incestuous love under the magnolia trees of an old plantation.

The secret was that Stella and the boy sometimes slept together. In retrospect, I can't think why it was such a secret, unless it was the boy's vanity that demanded they remain officially unattached. Their spotty, intermittent affair depended on him not seeing a more conventionally pretty girl, and was extremely damaging for Stella, who remained in a state of dramatically heightened jealousy at all times. There was a whiff of scandal to the whole thing, which came, in a world where surfaces were everything, from their being so mismatched in looks.

In other words, it was hardly an ambiguous situation. There was, Stella would later point out, no shortage of boys: there were boys with prettier eyes or a more refined knowledge of Proust; boys with more original neuroses, and less saccharine forms of spirituality. But the fact is that attractions are contagious. I spent hours sitting at Tommy's Lunch, drinking lime slushies and listening to Stella take apart the peculiarities of his character; hours listening to her fits of jealousy over the irresistible odalisques sprawled across his dorm bed. This is what happens when an overly intelligent woman brings all of her talents to bear on an infatuation: without either of us realizing what was happening, she somehow persuaded me of his attractiveness.

My flirtation with the boy, if you could even call it that, was beyond furtive. The three of us were often together, and he and I behaved toward each other with an irreproachable mixture of mannerliness and hostility. He came to visit me alone once when I was sick and brought me magazines and orange juice. Our conversation was innocent bordering on banal. I think we talked about the declining quality of the cereal selection at breakfast. Neither one of us told Stella about the visit.

And yet somehow we both knew. It was as abstract and agreed upon as an arranged marriage. I felt it when I stepped into the cool morning air, and gulped down a milky cup of coffee before class. I felt it when I walked next to the slate-colored river, watching the shallow crew boats skim the surface. It was with me, in other words, all the time: a low-grade excitement about this boy I barely knew. From this distance in time, this may be the most foreign and inscrutable part of the story: the attractions that could at any moment flare up and end your life as you knew it.

At this point I may as well offer a slight, very slight, argument in my defense: people didn't belong as absolutely to other people then. There was a kind of fluidity to our world. The barriers that in adult life seem so solid and fixed, literal walls defining your apartment, your bedroom, did not exist at that age. You listened, for instance, to your roommate having sex; you slept easily and deeply on someone else's couch; you ate breakfast, lunch, and dinner with everyone you knew. And somehow nothing was quite real unless it was shared, talked about, rehashed with friends, fretted about and analyzed, every single thing that happened, every minute gradation of emotion, more high-level gossip in the process of being told than events in and of themselves.

Over the summer the boy came to visit me in New York. I remember him standing in the doorway to my room, grinning, with an army-green duffel. Had we pretended it was a platonic

visit? It seems far-fetched that he would have come all the way
from New Hampshire to New York to see a casual acquaintance,
but I have a feeling that was what we told ourselves. We climbed
up to the roof of my parents' building and watched the boats go
by on the Hudson, the sun silhouetting the squat water towers a
dark silvery green.

I am aware, even now, of some small part of me that would
like to say that it was worth it, some adolescent, swaggering side
that would like to claim that the sexual moment itself seared the
imagination, and was worth, in its tawdry, obliterating way, the
whole friendship. It was not.

Of the act itself, I remember almost nothing at all. It seems
that when one is doing something truly illicit, not just moderately
illicit but plainly wrong, the sex itself is forgettable. The great
fact of the immorality overshadows anything two mere bodies
can achieve. All I remember is that he was gentle, in the way that
sensitive boys were supposed to be gentle. He brought me a warm
washcloth afterward, which sickened me slightly, and embarrassed me.

Stella, red pencil tucked behind her ear, would notice that I
haven't described the actual seduction. That I've looked politely
away from the events, because they are incriminating and, more
important, banal. I wouldn't want to debase my great betrayal,
my important, self-flagellating narrative, with anything so mundane as what actually happened. That's how she would see it,
anyway. Two people taking off their clothes, however gloriously
wrong, are, in the end, just two people taking off their clothes.

But really, the problem is that my mind has thrown up an elegant Japanese folding screen, with a vista of birds and mountains
and delicate, curling trees, to modestly block out the goings-on.

And it does seem after all of these years, that a blow-by-blow would be anticlimactic. I can say, in a larger sense, what happened, which is this: I didn't care about him, nor did I delude myself into thinking that I did. I had enough sense to know that what I was experiencing so forcefully was a fundamentally trivial physical impulse. And that's what makes the whole situation so bewildering and impenetrable. Why would one night with a boy I didn't even particularly like seem worth ruining a serious and irreplaceable friendship for?

I suppose, in accordance with the general and damaging abstraction of those years, I was fulfilling some misplaced idea of myself. I was finally someone who took things lightly. I thought a lot about "lightness" then. Even though I wasn't someone who took things lightly at all, I liked, that year, to think of myself as someone who did—all of which raises another question in my mind. Was at least part of the whole miserable escapade the fault of the Milan Kundera book everyone was reading, *The Unbearable Lightness of Being*? That sublime adolescent ode to emotional carelessness, that ubiquitous paperback expounding an obscure eastern European profundity in moral lapses? The more I think about it, the more I think it's fair to apportion a tiny bit of the blame to Mr. Kundera. (Here Stella would raise her eyebrows. "A book forced you to do it? How *literary* of you, how *well read* you must be. . . .")

I suppose, also, in some corner of my fevered and cowardly brain I must have thought we would get away with it. I must have thought we would sleep together once and get it out of our systems. It turned out, however, that the boy believed in "honesty," an approach I would not have chosen on my own. He called Stella at the soonest possible second and told her. It was not hard to imagine the frantic look in Stella's eyes when he told her. Stella looked frantic when she had to pour cornflakes in a bowl. I hated him for telling her. I couldn't bear the idea of her knowing. Strangely enough, I felt protective of her, as if I could somehow protect her from the threat of myself.

I don't think I grasped right away the magnitude of what I had done. It felt like waking up in the middle of a René Magritte painting and finding tiny men with bowler hats suddenly falling from the sky. It didn't make sense, even to me, and I was startled, in a way, to find that it was real. To have the boy in my house the next morning, wanting coffee, and to have his soft blue-and-green flannel shirt spread out on my floor, was for some reason extremely startling. Cause and effect were sufficiently severed in my mind that I had not apprehended the enormity of the betrayal. In the light of day, it seemed a little unfair that I couldn't take it back.

I don't remember if the boy called Stella from my house, or if he waited a few hours and called her from a phone booth in the train station. I do remember him reveling in his abject abasement. I couldn't believe how much he reveled. He was, among other things, a religious nut. But back to Stella. It's funny how even now my mind wanders back to him. This man I did not even delude myself into thinking that I cared about. This man I did not even *like*.

Stella, needless to say, was furious, mostly at me. I've noticed, in these cases, one is always furious at the person of the same sex, and one always finds the person of the other sex contemptible yet oddly blameless. To further complicate things, Stella and I were supposed to be roommates in the fall. This made everything infi-

nitely worse: undoing our roommate arrangements proved to be
more arduous than one would think. We had to disentangle ourselves officially in the eyes of the bureaucracy, and on paper: it
was like getting a divorce.

Before I go any further, maybe I should say something about
self-destructiveness in those years. That warm July night, there
was the pleasure of destruction, of Zippo lighters torching straw
huts, of razing something truly good and valuable to the ground;
there was the sense, however subliminal, of disemboweling a
friendship. I remember filleting fish that I caught with my father
on the docks, and seeing liver, kidney, roe, splayed open on the
slick wooden docks, for all to see. There was something thrilling
and disgusting about it. Tearing open my friendship with Stella
had the same effect. I felt sick. I felt the freeing thrill of ruining
everything.

And then again, it may be deceptive to talk about this whole
phase of life in terms of feeling. Maybe the problem was the absence of feeling. Maybe the problem was a kind of annihilating
rage that swept through me. Maybe I did what I did because, at
that age, I couldn't yet feel the way I wanted to feel, the way
Stella felt, about a man. A few lines of Wallace Stevens were
starred and highlighted in my Norton anthology: "Knows desire
without an object of desire, / All mind and violence and nothing
felt . . ."

From this vantage, the story is a little chilling. I would like to
say something in my defense, but what could I say? This is, by
its very nature, an act that cannot be defended. I will say that
my sense of morality shifted, that the last remnant of childhood,
that last puritanical streak of self-righteousness, vanished, that I

learned to be less rigid, because you never know. Fundamentally nice people have done deplorable things in their pasts. Fundamentally deplorable people change.

One could say that the seeds of the end of my friendship with Stella were embedded in the beginning. I met both her and the boy at once, after all; and I may have been attracted, in a way, to both of them at once, to the impossible, unwieldy triangle as it was being assembled. Stella may even have known, on the long nights the three of us spent together sitting around her fireplace, him slumped down on a chair, long legs gracefully crossed, listening to the whine of the Velvet Underground, that she was creating a problem; the temptation was that rooted, that inherent in the situation.

But back to the girl standing next to a tall boy by the water towers. The seconds before she leans into him, or he leans into her. The sky a glowing navy blue. How would the girl herself have explained? I am afraid that she would have come out with something like "It felt like the right thing." (I can hear Stella launch into this one: "It felt like the right thing. Of course it felt like the right thing. But did you stop to think for one second in the midst of all of this exalted feeling?") I am aware of how feeble this sounds, how predictable, how mundane, but I am trying to be as accurate as I can. In the moment it felt like one of those exceptional situations that rises above conventional morality, "in the moment" being another of those phrases one heard all the time back then. In the moment one is not thinking; in the moment the physical takes precedence; this is, of course, the businessman's excuse with his secretary, the politician's excuse with his intern, the tired cliché, in fact, of every single adulterer with the gall and the paltriness of spirit to try to explain himself, and yet it is true: in the moment, it did not feel as if there was a choice.

Afterward, I tried to wheedle my way back into Stella's affections. I had great faith in my wheedling back then. I wrote her a series of elaborately contrite letters. I remember quoting Auden in one of them: "In the deserts of the heart / Let the healing fountain start." But the heart remained a desert, as it tends to. Ornate apologies, overly flowery expressions of the self-contempt I did, in fact, feel, would not do. This, of course, is because nothing would do.

As it turned out, my efforts to explain myself bothered Stella to no end. I think, in retrospect, that all she wanted me to do was accept responsibility. I think the whole conversation about what happened exhausted her. Who cared why or how from her point of view? Who cared what particular frailties of character led me to be vulnerable to this sort of thing? What matters in the end is the irrevocable act. Even if I was able, through sheer force of will, to create a little ambiguity in a wholly unambiguous situation, there was something insulting, finally, about doing it. My impulse, it seemed, was to take the whole thing apart like a car motor, to take out the pieces and look at them together; of course, if I could engage her in this process, if I could get her to look at each one of these oily mechanisms *with* me, then I would be part of the way to regaining our friendship. It is the two of us doing something together, however awful. Stella, in her own way, sensed this and refused.

As for Stella, she hated me with aplomb. It was not a partial or forgiving hate. It was a deep, ardent hate. It was so seductive, this hate, that it pulled in other people who hated me too. Stella's

emotions were charismatic that way. There were whole tables in
the dining hall I had to avoid.

One could ask if I really wanted to save the friendship. I admit
that I might not have. I admit that there may have been something in the friendship that was crowding me. Why else would I
have done it? Why else did I have so few close women friends in
the first place? I have four sisters, and it may be that I already had
such an abundance of intense female love and ambivalence that
my friendships with women seemed just the tiniest bit disposable.
But this sort of psychoanalytic thinking has its limitations, especially when it comes to a nineteen-year-old. Because there may
have been something entirely accidental in the crash-up of the
friendship; it may have been a random act of violence, like someone taking out a gun in a school one day and shooting the principal's secretary.

I remember once when I was five my class was going on a trip
to Staten Island on a ferry. I had been looking forward to this trip
for weeks. The morning we were leaving, I had the signed permission slip from my parents. I had my cheese sandwich packed
in a paper bag, and my cardigan buttoned over my school uni-
form. And yet, when we got out onto the boardwalk, the wind
blowing from the East River, holding hands in twos, like the little
girls in the Madeline books, something happened. I started crying. The teacher stooped down, and I told her I had a stomach-
ache. I was sent home, and I missed the boat ride. Why had I
done it? my mother asked, somehow knowing that I was faking.
But I didn't know why: it was my first purely anarchic moment of
self-sabotage.

But then again, there *are* reasons that I could go into. There
are myriad possibilities as to why I would do something so pa-

tently absurd: I could go all the way back to Teddy Fairchild, the first boy I liked, with shoulder-length corn-colored hair, who left a bag of Russell Stover hard candies in my locker at camp, to my enormous shock, and then, at the end of the summer, never answered my letters. Or Henry Powers, who had café-latte-colored skin and dark curls, and decided, after our idyllic romps through the dunes on Nantucket, that he would rather play with boys. If I wanted to I could delve further into the great gaping insecurity that is always responsible for this sort of bad behavior: when I was thirteen I was very ill, and in and out of the hospital for a year. By the time it was clear I was going to be all right, I weighed sixty-two pounds. While my friends were cultivating the usual romantic dramas, I read books, and resigned myself to not being part of the game; and this resignation, this astonishment that a boy would like me, lingered dangerously. It turned me into something of a monster for a little while. Somehow this feeling that I was outside the romantic comings and goings of my peers got mingled with the idea that I wasn't going to live, that I was somehow outside of life. You can see where I am going with this. You can feel, in this explanation, the silent doctor nodding in the corner. So many exquisite explanations of appalling pieces of selfishness. And yet they are all true and not true; it may just have been a warm night and a beautiful boy.

If she were here now, Stella would say that all of this analyzing, all of this cyclical, wordy remorse, all of this endless trying to understand, or saying I'll never understand, all of this throwing up my hands in the face of human nature, or extolling the self-destructiveness of the age, is just another way of making this about me, rather than her. She would be right, of course: I am stealing the boy all over again.

PART II

Books

The Naked and the Conflicted

For a literary culture that fears it is on the brink of total annihilation, we are awfully cavalier about the Great Male Novelists of the last century. It has become popular to denounce those authors, and more particularly to deride the sex scenes in their novels. Even the young male writers who, in the scope of their ambition, would appear to be the heirs apparent have repudiated the aggressive virility of their predecessors.

After reading a sex scene in Philip Roth's latest novel, *The Humbling*, someone I know threw the book into the trash on a subway platform. It was not exactly feminist rage that motivated her. We have internalized the feminist critique pioneered by Kate Millett in *Sexual Politics* so completely that, as one of my students put it, "we can do the math ourselves." Instead, my acquaintance threw the book away on the grounds that the scene was disgusting, dated, redundant. But why, I kept wondering, did she have to throw it out? Did it perhaps retain a little of the provocative fire its author might have hoped for? Dovetailing with this private and admittedly limited anecdote, there is a punitive, vituperative quality in the published reviews that is always revealing of something larger in the culture, something beyond one aging writer's failure to produce fine enough sentences. All of which is to say: How is it possible that Philip Roth's sex scenes are still enraging us?

In the early novels of Roth and his cohort, there was in their dirty passages a sense of novelty, of news, of breaking out. Throughout the sixties, with books like *An American Dream*, *Herzog*, *Couples*, *Portnoy's Complaint*, and *Rabbit, Run*, there was a feeling that their authors were reporting from a new frontier of sexual behavior: adultery, anal sex, oral sex, threesomes—all of it had the thrill of the new, or at least of the newly discussed. When *Couples*, John Updike's tour de force of extramarital wanderlust set in a small New England town called Tarbox, came out in 1968, a *Time* cover article declared that "the sexual scenes, and the language that accompanies them, are remarkably explicit, even for this new age of total freedom of expression."

These novelists were writing about the bedrooms of middle-class life with the thrill of the censors at their backs, with the 1960 obscenity trial over *Lady Chatterley's Lover* fresh in their minds. They would bring their talent, their analytic insights, their keen writerly observation, to the most intimate, most unspeakable moments, and the exhilaration, the mischief, the crackling energy was in the prose. These young writers—Mailer, Roth, Updike— were taking up the X-rated subject matter of John O'Hara and Henry Miller, but with a dash of modern journalism splashed in.

In Philip Roth's phenomenally successful 1969 novel *Portnoy's Complaint*, the Jewish hero sleeps his way into mainstream America through the narrow loins of a series of crazy harridans and accommodating lovelies. But are the sex scenes meant to be taken seriously? In *The Counterlife*, Roth's alter ego, the writer Nathan

Zuckerman, calls himself a "sexual satirist," and in that book and others Roth's sex scenes do manage to be both comic and dirty at the same time: "The sight of the Zipper King's daughter sitting on the edge of the bathtub with her legs flung apart, wantonly surrendering all 5 feet 9 inches of herself to a vegetable, was as mysterious and compelling a vision as any Zuckerman had ever seen."

Roth's explicit passages walk a fine, difficult line between darkness, humor, and lust, and somehow the male hero emerges from all the comic clauses breathless, glorified. There is in these scenes rage, revenge, and some garden-variety sexism, but they are—in their force, in their gale winds, in their intelligence—charismatic, a celebration of the virility of their bookish, yet oddly irresistible, protagonists. As the best scenes spool forward, they are maddening, beautiful, eloquent, and repugnant all at once. One does not have to like Roth, or Zuckerman, or Portnoy, to admire the intensely narrated spectacle of their sexual adventures. Part of the suspense of a Roth passage, the tautness, the brilliance, the bravado, in the sentences themselves, the high-wire performance of his prose, is how infuriating and ugly and vain he can be without losing his readers (and then every now and then he actually goes ahead and loses them).

In 1960, the twenty-eight-year-old Updike solidified his emerging reputation as the author of eerily beautiful stories with his novel *Rabbit, Run*, about a lanky former basketball player turned kitchen utensil salesman, Harry (Rabbit) Angstrom, who runs off from his family, has sex with a plump and promiscuous mistress, and comes home to a wife who has drunkenly drowned their newborn baby. A few years later, Norman Mailer told Updike he should get back to the whorehouse and stop worrying about his prose style. But that was Updike's unnerving gift: to be frank and aestheticizing all at once, to do poetry *and* whorehouse. In *Couples,* a graphic description of oral sex includes "the floral surfaces of her mouth." In *Rabbit, Run,* we read of "lovely wobbly bubbles, heavy: perfume between. Taste, salt and sour, swirls back with his own saliva." The hallmark of Updike's sex scenes is the mingling of his usual brutal realism with a stepped-up rapture, a harsh scrutiny combined with prettiness. Everything is rose, milky, lilac, and then suddenly it is not.

For Rabbit, as for many Updike characters, sex offers an escape, an alternate life—a reprieve, even, in its finest moments, from mortality. In the *Time* cover story, Updike describes adultery as an "imaginative quest." In *Marry Me,* among other books, he expands on the theme that leaving one marriage for another doesn't resolve our deeper malaise, but he is interested in the motion, in the fantasy, in the impulse toward renewal: it is Rabbit running that he loves. As one of the characters in *Couples* puts it, adultery "is a way of giving yourself adventures. Of getting out in the world and seeking knowledge."

Saul Bellow shared Updike's interest in sexual adventuring, in a great, splashy, colorful comic-book war between men and women. Moses Herzog, he writes, "will never understand what women want. What do they want? They eat green salad and drink human blood." Bellow's novels are populated with dark, voluptuous, generous, maybe foreign Renatas and Ramonas, who are mistresses; and then there are the wives, shrewish, smart, treacherous, angular. While his sex scenes are generally more gentlemanly than those of Roth et al., he manages to get across something of his tussle with these big, fleshy, larger-than-life ladies: "Ramona had not learned those erotic monkey-shines in a manual, but in adventure, in confusion, and at times probably with a sinking heart, in brutal and often alien embraces."

In his disordered, sprawling novels, Mailer takes a hopped-up, quasi-religious view of sex, with flights of D. H. Lawrence–inspired mysticism and a special interest in sodomy. In *An American Dream*, he describes a woman's genitals: "It was no graveyard now, no warehouse, no, more like a chapel now, a modest decent place, but its walls were snug, its odor was green, there was a sweetness in the chapel."

Mailer's most controversial obsession is the violence in sex, the urge toward domination in its extreme. A sampling: "I wounded her, I knew it, she thrashed beneath me like a trapped little animal, making not a sound." "He must subdue her, absorb her, rip her apart and consume her." It is part of Mailer's existentialism, his singular, loopy philosophy, that violence is good, natural, and healthy, and it is this in his sex scenes that provokes. As in many of Mailer's ventures, like his famous campaign for mayor of New York, it's not entirely clear how much he means it and how much is for fun, for the virile show.

It would be too simple to call the explicit interludes of this new literature pornographic, as pornography has one purpose: to arouse. These passages are after several things at once—sadness, titillation, beauty, fear, comedy, disappointment, aspiration. The writers were interested in showing not just the triumphs of sexual conquest, but also its loneliness, its failures of connection. In his unruly defense of sexually explicit male literature in *The Prisoner of Sex*, Mailer wrote: "He has spent his literary life exploring the watershed of sex from that uncharted side which goes by the name of lust and it is an epic work for any man. . . . Lust exhibits all the attributes of junk. It dominates the mind and other habits, it appropriates loyalties, generalizes character, leaches character out, rides on the fuel of almost any emotional gas—whether hatred, affection, curiosity, even the pressures of boredom—yet it is never definable because it can alter to love or be as suddenly sealed from love."

In the intervening decades, the feminists objected; the public consumed; the novelists themselves were much decorated. And then somewhat to their surprise, the old guard got old. In books like Roth's *Exit Ghost* and Updike's *Toward the End of Time*, they began to take up the subject of impotence in various forms. Was it possible that the no-longer-young literary gods had fallen? Roth wrote in *Zuckerman Unbound:* "Life has its own flippant ideas about how to handle serious fellows like Zuckerman. All you have to do is wait and it teaches you all there is to know about the art of mockery."

And so we come back to the copy of *The Humbling* in the garbage can on the subway platform. The problem with the sex scenes in Philip Roth's late work is not that they are pornographic, but that they fail as pornography. One feels that the author's heart is not in it, that he is just going through the motions; one feels the impatient old master mapping out scenes (dildo, threesome), not writing them. The threesome in *The Humbling* has none of the quirkiness, the energy, the electric specificity, of the threesomes in *Portnoy's Complaint*, either the one where "the Monkey" eats a banana and gets her name, or the one where they pick up an Italian prostitute who later brings her son, all dressed up in his Sunday best, to see them. In the stripped-down later novels (*Everyman*, *Exit Ghost*, *Indignation*), Roth seems to have dispensed with the detail and idiosyncratic richness of his earlier work. As he writes about old men failing at sex, and raging about failing at sex, we see the old writer failing at writing about sex, which is, of course, a spectacle much more heartbreaking.

At this point, one might be thinking: Enter the young men, stage right. But our new batch of young or youngish male novelists are not dreaming up Portnoys or Rabbits. The current sexual style is more childlike; innocence is more fashionable than virility, the cuddle preferable to sex. Prototypical is a scene in Dave Eggers's road-trip novel, *You Shall Know Our Velocity*, where the hero leaves a disco with a woman and she undresses and climbs on top of him, and they just lie there: "Her weight was the ideal weight and I was warm and wanted her to be warm"; or the relationship in Benjamin Kunkel's *Indecision:* "We were sleeping together brother-sister style and mostly refraining from outright sex."

Characters in the fiction of the heirs apparent are often repelled or uncomfortable when faced with a sexual situation. In *Infinite Jest*, David Foster Wallace writes: "He had never once had actual intercourse on marijuana. Frankly, the idea repelled him. Two dry mouths bumping at each other, trying to kiss, his self-conscious thoughts twisting around on themselves like a snake on a stick while he bucked and snorted dryly above her." With another love interest, "his shame at what she might on the other hand perceive as his slimy phallocentric conduct toward her made it easier for him to avoid her, as well." Gone the familiar swagger, the straightforward artistic reveling in the sexual act itself. In Kunkel's version: "Maybe I was going to get lucky, something which, I reminded myself, following her up the stairs to our room and giving her ass a good review, wasn't always a piece of unmixed luck, and shouldn't automatically be hoped for any more than feared."

Rather than an interest in conquest or consummation, there is an obsessive fascination with trepidation, and with a convoluted, postfeminist second-guessing. Compare Kunkel's tentative and guilt-ridden masturbation scene in *Indecision* with Roth's famous onanistic exuberance with apple cores, liver, and candy wrappers in *Portnoy's Complaint*. Kunkel: "Feeling extremely uncouth, I put my penis away. I might have thrown it away if I could." Roth also writes about guilt, of course, but a guilt overridden and swept away, joyously subsumed in the sheer energy of taboo smashing: "How insane whipping out my joint like that! Imagine what would have been had I been caught red-handed! Imagine if I had gone ahead." In other words, one rarely gets the sense in Roth that he would throw away his penis if he could.

The literary possibilities of their own ambivalence are what beguile this new generation, rather than anything that takes place in the bedroom. In Michael Chabon's *Mysteries of Pittsburgh*, a woman in a green leather miniskirt and no underwear reads aloud from *Story of O*, and the protagonist says primly, "I refuse to flog you." In Jeffrey Eugenides's novel *The Marriage Plot*, his protagonist revises and corrects his own fantasy to make it less exploitative: "Mitchell felt guilty for fantasizing about his friend's girlfriend but not guilty enough to stop fantasizing. He didn't like what this fantasy of Claire on her knees in front of him said about him, so next he imagined himself generously going down on her."

For another exploration of guilt and ambivalence, take the following descriptions from Jonathan Franzen's novel *The Corrections:* "As a seducer, he was hampered by ambivalence." "He had, of course, been a lousy, anxious lover." "He could hardly believe she hadn't minded his attacks on her, all his pushing and pawing and poking. That she didn't feel like a piece of meat that he'd been using." And then the entire plot of Franzen's next novel, *Freedom,* is propelled by the extreme sensitivity of Patty's husband, Walter, whose relevant flaw is that he is too nice and decent and progressive to be compelling in bed. When Patty met him in college he called himself a feminist, and denounced misogynistic professors and said to her before they slept together, "I know essentially nothing about sex." In adult life, he blushes when embarrassed, and entertains thoughts like this: "Gender equality, as expressed in the pressure of Lalitha's neat foot on the gas pedal, made him glad to be alive in the twenty-first century." Patty marries him even though she is not sexually enthralled by him, and the events of the novel unfold from there. (And then, of course, there are writers like Jonathan Safran Foer who avoid the corruptions of adult sexuality by choosing children and virgins as their protagonists.)

The same crusading feminist critics who objected to Mailer, Bellow, Roth, and Updike might be tempted to take this new sensitivity or softness or indifference to sexual adventuring as a sign of progress (Mailer called these critics "the ladies with their fierce ideas"). But the sexism in the work of the heirs apparent is simply wilier and shrewder and harder to smoke out. What comes to mind is Franzen's description of one of his female characters in *The Corrections:* "Denise at 32 was still beautiful." To the esteemed ladies of the movement I would suggest this is not how our Great Male Novelists would write in the feminist utopia.

The younger writers are so self-conscious, so steeped in a certain kind of liberal education, that their characters can't condone even their own sexual impulses; they are, in short, too cool for sex. Even the mildest display of male aggression is a sign of being overly hopeful, overly earnest or politically untoward. For a character to feel himself, even fleetingly, a conquering hero is somehow passé. More precisely, for a character to attach too much importance to sex, or aspiration to it, to believe that it might be a force that could change things, and possibly for the better, would be hopelessly retrograde. Passivity, a paralyzed sweetness, a deep ambivalence about sexual appetite, are somehow taken as signs of a complex and admirable inner life. These are writers in love with irony, with the literary possibility of self-consciousness so extreme it almost precludes the minimal abandon necessary for the sexual act itself, and in direct rebellion against the Roth, Updike, and Bellow their college girlfriends denounced. (Recounting one such denunciation, David Foster Wallace says a friend called Updike "just a penis with a thesaurus.")

This generation of writers is suspicious of what Michael Chabon, in *Wonder Boys*, calls "the artificial hopefulness of sex." They are good guys, sensitive guys, and if their writing is denuded of a certain carnality, if it lacks a sense of possibility, of expansiveness, of the bewildering, transporting effects of physical love, it is because of a certain cultural shutting down, a deep, almost puritanical disapproval of their literary forebears and the shenanigans they lived through.

In a vitriolic attack on Updike's *Toward the End of Time*, David Foster Wallace said of the novel's narrator, Ben Turnbull, that "he persists in the bizarre adolescent idea that getting to have sex with whomever one wants whenever one wants is a cure for ontological despair," and that Updike himself "makes it plain that he views the narrator's impotence as catastrophic, as the ultimate symbol of death itself, and he clearly wants us to mourn it

as much as Turnbull does. I'm not especially offended by this attitude; I mostly just don't get it."

In this same essay, Wallace goes on to attack Updike and, in
passing, Roth and Mailer for being narcissists. But does this mean
that the new generation of novelists is not narcissistic? I would
suspect, narcissism being about as common among male novelists
as brown eyes in the general public, that it does not. It means that
we are simply witnessing the flowering of a new narcissism: boys
too busy gazing at themselves in the mirror to think much about
girls, boys lost in the beautiful vanity of "I was warm and wanted
her to be warm," or the noble purity of being just a tiny bit repelled by the crude advances of the desiring world.

After the sweep of the last half century, our bookshelves look
different than they did to the young Kate Millett, drinking her
nightly martini in her downtown apartment, shoring up her cour-
age to take great writers to task in *Sexual Politics* for the ways in
which their sex scenes demeaned, insulted, or oppressed women.
These days the revolutionary attitude may be to stop dwelling
on the drearier aspects of our more explicit literature. In contrast
to their cautious, entangled, ambivalent, endlessly ironic heirs,
there is something almost romantic in the old guard's view of
sex: it has a mystery and a power, at least. It makes things happen.

Kate Millett might prefer that Norman Mailer have a different
taste in sexual position, or that Bellow's fragrant ladies bear
slightly less resemblance to one another, or that Rabbit not sleep
with his daughter-in-law the day he comes home from heart surgery, but one can't deny that there is in these old paperbacks an
abiding interest in the sexual connection.

Compared with the new purity, the self-conscious paralysis,
the self-regarding ambivalence, Updike's notion of sex as an

"imaginative quest" has a certain vanished grandeur. The fluidity of Updike's Tarbox, with its boozy volleyball games and adulterous couples copulating alfresco, has disappeared into the Starbucks lattes and minivans of our current suburbs, and our towns and cities are more solid, our marriages safer; we have landed upon a more conservative time. Why, then, should we be bothered by our literary lions' continuing obsession with sex? Why should it threaten our insistent modern cynicism, our stern belief that sex is no cure for what David Foster Wallace called "ontological despair"? Why don't we look at these older writers, who want to defeat death with sex, with the same fondness as we do the inventors of the first, failed airplanes, who stood on the tarmac with their unwieldy, impossible machines, and looked up at the sky?

Writing Women

It may be surprising that there's been no comprehensive history of women's writing in America, but Elaine Showalter has undertaken this daunting venture with her vast democratic volume, *A Jury of Her Peers: American Women Writers from Anne Bradstreet to Annie Proulx*, in which she energetically describes the work of long-forgotten writers and poets along with that of their more well-known contemporaries. In the 1970s, Showalter wrote *A Literature of Their Own: British Women Novelists from Brontë to Lessing*, which established an alternative canon of British women writers at a moment when feminist studies were very much in vogue, and her new book is an attempt to do the same thing for American literature. Showalter was, for nearly two decades, a professor in the department of English literature at Princeton (she was the head of the department when I was a graduate student there), and she remains a grande dame of feminist literary studies.

It's worth noting that many of the most talented writers she discusses—Edith Wharton, Willa Cather, Mary McCarthy, Elizabeth Bishop, Joan Didion—objected to being categorized as women writers and preferred to think of themselves simply as writers. As Elizabeth Bishop put it, "art is art and to separate writings, paintings, musical compositions, etc., into two sexes is to emphasize values that are not art." Showalter handles these rebels by corralling them into special subchapters with titles like "Dissenters." One of the dissenters, Cynthia Ozick, argued against expecting "artists who are women . . . to deliver 'women's art,' as if 10,000 other possibilities, preoccupations, obsessions, were inauthentic, for women, or invalid, or worse yet, lyingly evasive."

A Jury of Her Peers announces its inclusiveness with its size and heft, and the breadth of Showalter's research is indeed impressive; it seems there are women scribblers under every apple tree, in every city street and small-town café across our great nation. In fact, the encyclopedic nature of the book is both its satisfaction and its limitation. The entries are brisk, informative, and often less than a page long. There are too many writers here to go into much depth about any of them, and one finds oneself, in many of the more absorbing passages of the book, wanting more. Of course, distilling any writer's lifework into a brief entry entails a certain amount of glossing over. To cover so much territory necessitates a kind of breezy simplification, and that very breezy simplification is also the pleasure of this kind of ranging, inclusive history.

Although she refers to *A Jury of Her Peers* as literary history, Showalter is less attentive to artistic merit, to what separates good fiction from bad, than to cultural significance; she is less concerned with the nuances of style or art than with the political ramifications of a book, or the spirited or adventurous behavior of its lady characters. Like other feminist scholars of her ilk, she is not interested in whether the writers she discusses are good *writers*, or in the question of how their best writing works, but in whether they are exploring feminist themes. And so she ends up rooting through novels and poems for messages and meanings about women's position in society, for plots that criticize domesticity or that expound on the narrowness of women's lives. (She once coined the term "gynocritic" for critics freed "from the linear absolutes of male literary history.") This exploration of subversive plots and spunky heroines may be fruitful from a purely historical or political point of view, but it doesn't always feel like literary criticism at its most sophisticated. One thinks of Joan Didion's line about feminists: "That fiction has certain irreducible ambiguities seemed never to occur to these women, nor should it have, for fiction is in most ways hostile to ideology."

Showalter is occasionally prone to bouts of reductionist readings that belong to a faded era of bell-bottoms and consciousness-raising groups, as when she declares the intricately drawn characters Gus Trenor, Percy Gryce, and Simon Rosedale in Edith Wharton's *House of Mirth* to be "products of their own crisis of gender," or when she writes that Sylvia Plath's richly nuanced poem "Daddy" "embodied women's rejection of patriarchal mythologies." But on the whole her writing is clear and lively and mercifully free of the fashionable jargon of academic criticism.

Showalter's wide net draws in writers like Dorothy Canfield Fisher, whose novel *The Home-Maker*, written in 1924, includes the abysmally written passage: "What was her life? A hateful round of housework, which, hurry as she might, was never done. How she loathed housework! The sight of a dishpan full of dishes made her feel like screaming. And what else did she have? Lone-

liness; never-ending monotony; blank, gray days, one after another full of drudgery." Very few people, I imagine, would argue
for the elegance of the prose, but the passage is undoubtedly interesting from a feminist point of view. And so the question becomes: Is this capacious, political way of looking at writing a
flawed way to approach the mysteries of literature? Willa Cather
put it this way: "The mind that can follow a 'mission' is not an
artistic one."

Showalter's final section on modern women writers, with
headings like "From Chick Lit to Chica Lit," is the flimsiest in the
book. Where, one wonders, are some of the quirkier and more
interesting talents of the past few decades, from Paula Fox to
Mary Gaitskill to Claire Messud? Showalter spends too much
time on frothy entertainments like Jennifer Weiner's *Good in Bed*
and Terry McMillan's *Waiting to Exhale* at the expense of more
serious work.

Toward the end of this ambitious book, Showalter concludes
that one "must be willing to assume the responsibility of judging.
A peer is not restricted to explaining and admiring; quite the con-
trary." But one wishes there was more judgment in this book,
more selection. The idea of resurrecting women's writing from
the neglect of previous eras is a natural project emanating from
1970s feminism, but is the mere fact of being a woman and jotting
down words in a notebook and then publishing them worthy of
quite so many drums and trumpets? It may not be sensitive to say
that some, just some, of the writers in this generous volume
might have rightfully been relegated to obscurity, but one can't
help thinking, at times, that literary history may have passed
them over for a reason, just as it has passed over mediocre, or
truly terrible, male writers.

One also wonders about the sheer democracy of the project, the fair-minded curiosity about nearly every woman who thought to pick up a pen. Does Dorothy Canfield Fisher really merit as much space as Elizabeth Bishop? It is a vexed and knotty question: Is Showalter in some way devaluing the achievements of the greatest American writers by giving equal or greater space to the less talented? Is she slighting women writers by holding them to a standard that is not about artistic excellence, but about the political content or personal drama of their writing? In her brilliant essay "Silly Novels by Lady Novelists," George Eliot wrote, "The severer critics are fulfilling a chivalrous duty in depriving the mere fact of feminine authorship of any false prestige which may give it a delusive attraction, and in recommending women of mediocre faculties—as at least a negative service they can render their sex—to abstain from writing."

Still, this comprehensive record of American women's attempts at literary achievement holds its own fascination; the small, vivid portraits of women's lives are extremely readable and enlightening. Writing about times when women's stories were too often ignored, Showalter offers a series of vignettes about what their struggles consisted of and how difficult it was for a woman to forge a professional identity as a writer. She is concerned with the drama of women writing; the lives she describes are filled with abortions, divorces, affairs, unhappy marriages, postpartum depressions, and suicides. Her short, incisive biographies offer a glimpse into the exotic travails of the past and the eternal concerns of female experience; and of course, from a purely biographical standpoint the literary mediocrities can be as interesting as the successes.

A Jury of Her Peers is likely to become an important and valu-

able resource for anyone interested in women's history. It out-
lines the rich and colorful history of women struggling to publish
and define themselves, and the complex and tangled tradition of
women's writing in this country. It also leaves us with many
memorable moments, like Dorothy Parker praying, "Dear God,
please make me stop writing like a woman."

The Bratty Bystander

The biographies of great writers have been slowly overshadowed by the biographies of bystanders—usually female bystanders. These biographies interest themselves not with women who wrote great books, but with women who happened to be standing there as they were being written, women like Zelda Fitzgerald, Vera Nabokov, Georgie Yeats, Vivienne Eliot, and Nora Joyce. The latest engrossing contribution to the genre is Carol Shloss's *Lucia Joyce: To Dance in the Wake*. Once the genre served as an original, quirky feminist corrective, but now, as it becomes more prevalent, it panders to a culture more enamored of prurient gossip than of literature itself.

The premise of *Lucia Joyce*, like the rest of these biographies, is that the woman is an artist herself. The Great Man is not creating by himself, but somehow channeling the energies of the women around him. James Joyce's daughter, Lucia, was a dancer. "She too had been an artist," Shloss informs us, "who worked with a fervor and vision comparable to Joyce's own." Her accomplishments, in addition to dancing, were apparently a novel that's been lost and a few illustrations. But Shloss's evidence of her genius seems to be gleaned from her imitations of Charlie Chaplin at parties, a photograph of a dance performance in which she wore a sensational, mirrored, fish costume, and "excellent report cards" from her childhood.

Lucia herself felt quite rivalrous with her father. When friends called Joyce to congratulate him on winning his obscenity trial in the United States, enabling the publication of *Ulysses,* Lucia cut the phone wire, saying, "I am the artist!" It's unclear whether this episode comes out of craziness or theater. Later, she behaves in ways that seem more clearly mad: she sets fires, throws a chair at her mother, unzips the pants of male visitors, sleeps with the gas on, sends telegrams to dead people, and wanders through Dublin for days, sleeping on the street.

Inevitably, these progressive new biographies conflate brattiness, mental imbalance, and brilliance into a miasma of thwarted ability. One of the hallmarks of the woman-attached-to-great-men genre is that the Great Man has somehow prevented the female family member from achieving her potential. In this case, Joyce spirited his gifted daughter to London away from Paris, where, after years of dilettantish wandering, joining and quitting dance groups that sound suspiciously like cults, she somehow miraculously had been about to find her calling. He wouldn't let her dance, and thus crushed her spirit. You may not be altogether surprised to hear that other male villains lurk in the margins: there are male artists like Samuel Beckett and Alexander Calder who sleep with Lucia and abandon her. There is also a brother who Shloss suggests—with astonishingly little evidence—may have sexually abused her, and seems ferociously bent on keeping her in an institution, so that she won't tell the story of this abuse.

No matter how sensationalized the life, our appetite for these biographies is enormous. And there is no denying that the book is monumentally engaging, but why? We find something reassuring about the stories of the almost-artist, the brilliant "fantastic being," who could have written *Ulysses* but somehow never got around to it. The ordinary woman, the daughter, wife, mother, who people remember sparkling in conversation or wearing a particularly beautiful dress, is elevated to the status of artist. In a way, Lucia Joyce is the ultimate heroine of this genre—a dancer who doesn't dance, a painter who doesn't paint, *and* a writer who doesn't write. Shloss writes, "Lucia spoke in a kind of body language that expressed pain and suffering and unspoken desires. She expressed life as a dance of false starts and small triumphs, of emotions lifted, of hopes deflated."

Women readers, in particular, are endlessly drawn to these stories of doom and raw talent. It confirms some view we have of the world that is not nurturing our talent; it shifts the responsibility from us onto the shadowy male world. It taps into the secret biography of our innermost aspirations, the half-written screenplays in our computers, the proverbial novels in drawers. But why have we been thwarted? Has someone physically prevented us from writing *Ulysses*, or are we just not talented or driven enough? The comforting, democratic message of these books is that you don't have to write or paint or act to be "an artist." It is enough to *be*. To Shloss, "Lucia didn't need books like *Ulysses* to become modern."

Of course, the biographies of great men's women lend themselves to all kinds of romanticizing. It is, in these hefty, attractive books, with their dramatic sepia covers, enormously glamorous to be mad. Had Lucia Joyce simply married, and stayed in Paris and taught dance to eager young protégées, and pursued her art in a modest way, and grown fat and happy and had a couple of children in a little apartment with a view of the river, there would be no *Lucia Joyce: To Dance in the Wake.*

In spite of its romantic frisson, the position of muse is very vague and largely thankless for the muse herself. It would be nice to think that *Ulysses* or *Finnegans Wake* could not have been written without Lucia; but of course, one suspects that they could have been. In this case, Lucia's role as muse seems to consist of a single afternoon where she was dancing in a room where Joyce happened to be writing *Finnegans Wake:* "There are two artists in his room, and both of them are working. Joyce is watching and learning . . . the place where she meets her father is not in consciousness but in some more primitive place before consciousness." This is a pretty image, and Shloss embellishes it even further: "They understand each other, for they speak the same language, a language not yet arrived into words and concepts, but a language nonetheless, founded on the communicative body."

And what about Lucia herself, petulant, mesmerizing, fragile, bratty Lucia? She liked to sleep outside under the stars, and walk around without underwear, and swim in the middle of the night. Instead she spent fifty-odd years in an institution. There is no poetry, no glory, in this story, no secret communion, no mystical collaboration, no intangible collusion, between father and daughter, only pointless, run-of-the-mill human suffering. Instead of the subtle literary pas de deux between Joyce and his daughter, the truth is more painful and nonsensical: a woman's life was wasted. Books like this give a dishonest, literary gloss to what is a form of illicit voyeurism; they free us from the difficulty of literature into the easy glamour of being vaguely associated with it, and deploy the language and cachet of feminism to celebrate those moments when women are not writing or painting or otherwise creating.

Reclaiming the Shrew

Few endeavors would appear as arduous and maddening to a responsible scholar as a biography of Shakespeare's wife, Ann Hathaway. We have almost no solid facts about Mrs. Shakespeare's life, and we know almost nothing about the Shakespeares' marriage. We know that the playwright could have brought his wife to live with him in London and did not, though we don't know how often he made the three-day trip back to Stratford. We know that in his will, he left his wife only his "second-best bed."

From this slender evidence, along with liberal and dubious readings of the plays and sonnets, scholars have created a robust portrait of the Shakespeares' unhappy domestic life—a "marriage of evil auspices," as one scholar put it. Rather than inhibiting biographers, the lack of information seems to have freed many of them to project their own blooming fantasies onto the relationship. The prevailing image of Ann Hathaway is that of an illiterate seductress who beguiled the young Shakespeare, conceived a child, and ensnared him in a loveless union. Germaine Greer's task in her ingenious new book, *Shakespeare's Wife*, is to expose the construction of this fantasy, tracing its evolution from early biographers like Thomas de Quincey through the work of respected modern scholars like Stephen Greenblatt. "The Shakespeare wallahs," she writes, "have succeeded in creating a Bard in their own likeness, that is to say, incapable of relating to women."

After sifting through records of lives that ran parallel to the young Shakespeares', Greer contends that in their time and place there was nothing unusual in a baby's being born six months after a marriage. She also demonstrates that an unmarried woman in her mid-twenties would not have been considered exceptional or desperate. Ann Hathaway, Greer argues, was likely to be literate, and given the relative standing of their families in Warwickshire, she may very well have been considered a more desirable match than her husband.

Though generally appreciative, several Shakespeare scholars have found Greer's approach "stridently . . . combative" and full of "scattergun assaults." But for those accustomed to Greer's feminist provocations, *Shakespeare's Wife* will seem extremely sober and restrained. Rarely have the possibilities of the conditional tense been so fully exploited: the entire book is written in elaborately tentative lines like "she may have permitted herself the odd grim little smile" and "he might have read them out to her." Greer has a doctorate in Elizabethan drama from Newnham College, Cambridge, and she is almost showy in her research into parish registers, in her dry apprehension of fact. Germaine Greer, it turns out, is an unusual type, with both a polemicist's vision and a scholar's patience. In spite of her flamboyant reputation, she has never resorted to the easy or the doctrinaire. *The Female Eunuch* (1971), her brilliant analysis of women's oppression, was mischievous, restless, wide-ranging, unpredictable. Of the nonfiction classics of 1970s feminism, hers alone eluded the imaginative limits and rigidity of good politics. *Shakespeare's Wife* similarly transcends the drab conventions of much academic excavation of lost female figures.

Even within the context of Shakespeare studies, however, Greer's speculations are, for the most part, surprisingly responsible. Many of her more fanciful theories, like the possibility that Shakespeare died of syphilis, are shared by more mainstream scholars. Because so little about the playwright's life is known, prejudice and desire assume a greater role than in most biography. The biographer is forced to create his or her own version of Shakespeare, and Greer is no exception.

Inevitably, in imagining the Shakespeares' marriage, Greer draws heavily on archetypes from her own work. Her Ann Hathaway is unusually independent and hardworking. She is almost too good to be true, and she is certainly too good to be interesting. "Though Ann Hathaway had been living manless for nearly 30 years," Greer writes in a chapter on Shakespeare's return from London around 1611, "no breath of scandal ever attached to her name, which, given the evidence of the surviving records of the Vicar's Court, is itself remarkable." In Greer's view, Shakespeare did not support his wife financially, and during his long absences she devoted herself to running a malt business or otherwise taking care of her children.

If Greer consistently romanticizes anything, it is female independence. While acknowledging the complexity and drama of sex, Greer has long celebrated the woman who lives apart, who somehow evades the ordinary encumbrances of a man in her daily life. She devotes an entire section of *The Female Eunuch* to alternatives to the oppressions of the nuclear family and quotes a sociologist from the 1930s: "For a male and female to live continuously together is . . . biologically speaking, an extremely unnatural condition." One can hear Greer's feminist interpretations beneath her descriptions of Hathaway's life. Ann "could have been confident of her ability to support herself and her children, but not if she had also to deal with a layabout husband good for nothing but spinning verses," she writes in a chapter suggesting that Ann may well have encouraged Shakespeare to go to London. Her observation that "when her husband died Ann was 60, and free for the first time in a third of a century" evokes another line from an earlier book, *The Change:* "To be unwanted is also to be free." At times, one suspects that Greer is writing more about an idea of freedom than about any historical woman.

Toward the end of *Shakespeare's Wife,* Greer makes the implausible case that Ann was responsible for the publication of the First Folio in 1623. Here one may recall Tom Wolfe's account of a younger Greer at a dinner party, getting bored and setting fire to her hair. And yet it often seems that Greer is slyly drawing attention to the novelist's endeavor, that she is self-consciously pointing out the element of fiction writing inherent in any effort to understand Shakespeare's life. She playfully begins each chapter with summaries reminiscent of nineteenth-century novels. And she writes that the book is "heresy, and probably neither truer nor less true than the accepted prejudice." Does it matter if Greer's theories are true? In spinning her version, she has opened up the story; she has laid bare the fantasies, uprooted the assumptions. It's unlikely that hereafter the shadowy figure in the corner of the great house in Stratford will be treated with the same easy contempt.

One might wonder why this book, filled with mundane ac-

counts of business deals, wills, and birth records, is so riveting. It
may be that one senses the passion in the archives, in the artifacts
of daily life that Greer meticulously uncovers. In her research
into the life of another widow in Stratford, Greer finds: "In all,
her possessions were worth £17 10s 2d, of which £4 was in wheat
and barley. She too owned her own pewter and brass, and five
flitches of bacon, probably of her own curing, for in her barn
there were two 'store pigs,' as well as a cow and a heifer, two
geese and a gander, 12 hens and a cock. It seems that right up to
her last days Elizabeth supported herself by selling her butter and
eggs and bacon." The details—so rare, so tangible—have the
bareness of poetry. The world of Elizabethan England is so completely lost to us that these hard facts glow a little in the darkness.

In *A Room of One's Own*, with its famous riff on Shakespeare's
sister, Virginia Woolf wrote that when one tries to picture the life
of an Elizabethan woman, "one is held up by the scarcity of facts.
One knows nothing detailed, nothing perfectly true and substan-
tial about her. History scarcely mentions her. . . . What one wants,
I thought—and why does not some brilliant student at Newnham
or Girton supply it?—is a mass of information; at what age did
she marry; how many children had she as a rule; . . . did she do the
cooking; would she be likely to have a servant? All these facts lie
somewhere, presumably, in parish registers and account books;
the life of the average Elizabethan woman must be scattered
about somewhere, could one collect and make a book of it. It
would be ambitious beyond my daring." And now the book written by a brilliant student from Newnham, dreamed of by Virginia
Woolf in the last century, exists: lively, rigorous, fiercely imagined.

Making the Incest Scene

All unhappy families may have been unhappy in their own fashion in the days when Tolstoy wrote the famous opening lines of *Anna Karenina*, but today's unhappy families—at least in fiction—seem pretty much the same. It often happens that I am in a bookstore leafing through one of the attractive new hardcovers, when my eye catches a phrase on the inside jacket: "until she is forced to come to terms with the dark secret of her harrowing past." I know without reading any further what the dark secret is, and my heart sinks: *another novel about incest.*

Sexual abuse, of course, is everywhere splashed across the culture, wept about on talk shows, endlessly reported in the news, and writers of fiction have obligingly followed suit; incest has become our latest literary vogue. We are deluged with descriptions of fathers taking their daughters on their laps and sliding their hands under their skirts or creeping into their bedrooms in the middle of the night. These images appear not only in best-selling books like Stephen King's *Gerald's Game* but also in the quieter pages of what we consider serious literary fiction, books that win Pulitzer Prizes and National Book Critics Circle Awards, like Jane Smiley's *A Thousand Acres*. Here the ancient theme of *Oedipus Rex* is accompanied by the clattering breakfast plates of twentieth-century realism and the tragic, shimmering myth becomes an actual event described in pornographic detail. As any consumer of current fiction will notice, our bookshelves are filled with stories of the family romance getting a little too romantic: Donna Tartt's *The Secret History*, E. Annie Proulx's *The Shipping News*, Amy Bloom's *Come to Me*, Dorothy Allison's *Bastard Out of Carolina*, Joyce Carol Oates's *You Must Remember This*, Heather Lewis's *House Rules*, Margaret Atwood's *The Robber Bride*, Marilyn French's *Our Father*, Mary Gaitskill's *Two Girls, Fat and Thin*, Geoffrey Wolff's *The Age of Consent*, Anne Rice's *The Witching Hour*, Josephine Hart's *Damage*, and Russell Banks's *The Sweet Hereafter*, to name only a few.

One of the most talked-about bidding wars in the publishing world this year was not over a new thriller by Michael Crichton or John Grisham but over a half-written first novel by an unknown female poet who calls herself Sapphire. "I was left back when I was twelve because I had a baby for my fahver [*sic*]," the unpublished manuscript of *Push* begins.* Set in the projects of Harlem, the story reveals a teenage girl who is sexually abused not just by her father but by her obese mother as well. Sapphire announces, "We is a nation of raped children." Whatever the truth of that, we are certainly a nation that wants to read about them.

Of course, every generation of writers pursues the mirage of the zeitgeist. In the twenties, writers became enamored with dis-

---

* Her character would many years later be popularized and picked up in the movie *Precious*. Sapphire is no longer recognizable as the "unknown female poet" she was at the time I wrote this essay.

affected Americans in Europe, and in the thirties they discovered migrant workers and tenement dwellers. In the sixties they became obsessed with psychiatrists and neuroses, and in the eighties they found revelation in drugs and urban anomie. Each decade a batch of novels are announced as electric, explosive, original, articulate of our most pressing concerns. But zeitgeist fiction works like a newspaper. Most of the books that seemed so new, so relevant, so absolutely of the moment, fade. We are left with the best of these books, which are good not because they are about the subject everyone was discussing that year but in spite of it.

The current trend, it seems, blew north from the hot porches of Southern literature. The heirs of the gothic imaginations of writers like William Faulkner and Erskine Caldwell appeared at first to be mostly black women writers. The graphic sexual abuse in Toni Morrison's *The Bluest Eye* (1970) and Maya Angelou's *I Know Why the Caged Bird Sings* (1971) offered the prototypes for the modern incest scene. After that came Alice Walker's *The Color Purple* (1982), with the memorable incestuous moment—"he put his thing up gainst my hip and sort of wiggle it around"—on the first page. Then, in the eighties, the alchemy of academia and politics created a mainstream fascination with victims of all kinds; the concurrent rise of a certain pop-feminist sensibility made sexual victims particularly compelling—even requisite. By the early nineties, incest had swept across the literary map of America—into Mona Simpson's California cities, Jane Smiley's flat Midwestern farmlands, Mary Gaitskill's middle-class suburbs, Russell Banks's small upstate New York towns, and even E. Annie Proulx's icy Canadian islands.

Novelists, we know, have been fascinated by incest for almost as long as there have been novels: in 1722, Daniel Defoe's racy heroine Moll Flanders discovers that the man she is happily married to is actually her brother. But in the glare of all the television lights and cameras focused on sexual abuse and recovered memory, today's incest scenes have an unmistakably current feel. "Why is there this empty place in my memory?" writes Marilyn French in her novel *Our Father,* her prose virtually vibrating with timeliness. A hundred pages later it turns out that there is an "empty place" in Alex's memory because her rich and politically powerful father molested her when she was in diapers. As the eighty-two-year-old patriarch lies in a coma, Alex and her three sisters, one of whom is the illegitimate daughter of the maid, gather together in his mansion and discover that he has had sex with all of them, as well as with one of his granddaughters. "It was so awful! It hurt and I didn't want it!" exclaims one of the sisters. In the climactic scene of disclosure, the story merges with something we just read in *People* or a scandal we just saw on the local news. The writer raises her voice to the ecstatic confessional pitch of *Oprah* and borrows the easy intimacy of that medium.

Smiley's critically acclaimed *A Thousand Acres* is the most prominent example of the new genre. In it, Smiley gives us a sixteenth-century drama with a twentieth-century twist: a sexually abusive *King Lear* set in the pastoral cornfields of modern Iowa. This time around, the daughters, Ginny and Rose, have every reason to be angry at their strong-willed father. When they were young, the respected pillar of the community entered their yellow-and-pink-flowered bedrooms and had sex with them. Rose remembers and Ginny forgets. On finding out the dark secret, the reader is supposed to think with satisfaction, *Oh yes, now it all falls into place:* Ginny's passivity, Rose's hardness, their fear and anger and cruelty, their putting their father out in the furious storm—all make perfect sense. But what the reader really feels is frustration at the spectacle of a skillful writer using such a cheap trick: it's terrible to watch the potential grandeur of the book, the daughters' greed and bitterness, and all of the eternal mysteries of the Lear story collapse into such a politically trendy and prosaically simple solution.

If in *A Thousand Acres* incest works as a kind of bargain-basement epiphany, Smiley is not alone. In *Our Father*, *The Age of Consent*, *House Rules*, and countless other novels, the entire story is reduced to a riddle, and incest is the answer. The riddle goes something like this: Mary or Maisie or Rose is acting kind of strange. She is fat or promiscuous or bitter or she dives headfirst into a shallow pond, and it turns out, many pages later, that Mary or Maisie or Rose was molested as a child by her father or stepfather or father figure. The discovery of the central fact is like a flash of lightning illuminating the entire book.

We have come to expect psychological lightning from the books we read on beaches and buses and trains. We want motives, symptoms, childhood traumas. We want years on the analyst's couch condensed into a single paragraph. We want the deep pleasure of what reviewers call "penetrating psychological insight," but we don't, it would appear, want to work too hard for it. Novels like Smiley's offer the perfect solution—the therapeutic thrill of delving into the past combined with the convenience of prepackaged interpretation: one overarching explanation for everything that's gone wrong. Such books operate on the idea, borrowed from talk shows, that the complexity of human character must be presented, analyzed, and solved in the space of one hour, not including commercials.

Is the subject of incest, then, inherently cheap? Not necessar-

ily. But the situation itself is so extreme that it grabs our interest
with very little skill on the part of the writer—like a murder or a
car crash, it jolts us into the story. As the father reaches under his
daughter's nightgown, we can't help but be fascinated. Amy
Bloom may be a talented writer, but when she writes about a
mother having sex with her stepson she doesn't really have to be;
she gets our attention anyway. A Freudian would say that seeing
this subconscious stuff dramatized appeals to our most primal
fears and fantasies. Whatever the appeal, the situation itself, as in
the following instance from Mary Gaitskill's *Two Girls, Fat and
Thin,* demands our sympathy:

> He pulled me against him, crushing my face into the chest
> hairs exposed by his open pajama top. I felt the power and
> insistence in his embrace, felt how tight were the muscles
> of his embracing arm. . . . I put out my hands and clutched
> his pajamas in my fists. "Yes," he said, his voice crushed
> and strange. "Yes." He moved his hand away from my
> chest, not loosening his grip on my shoulders. Through
> the gown, he touched between my legs. Shock impaled my
> body.

Gaitskill's words are forceful. You have to feel horror, and the
breathless panic of the thirteen-year-old being molested by her
father. Gaitskill continues: "My flannel gown scrunched up
around my shoulders and my buttocks rubbed by what felt like
the blunt, hairless limb of a medium-sized animal." Because of
the nature of the crime, the characters tend to be separated in
crude shorthand: father, evil; daughter, innocent. The girl with
her nightgown scrunched up over her shoulders versus "the

blunt, hairless limb of a medium-sized animal." Because the drama is so literal, we get none of the play of the shadowy tensions in, say, *Hamlet*, none of the everyday tangle of ambiguities, hopes, pleasures, disillusionments, depressions of a novel by an author like John Updike, who writes about the human world in all of its radiant confusion.

There is, nonetheless, something tough and appealing about writers like Gaitskill, Simpson, and Allison writing about the traditional domestic scene in a way that Louisa May Alcott would never have dreamed of doing. At their best, books about incest have, like Allison's *Bastard Out of Carolina*, the irreverent, anarchic energy that comes from exposing one's family of origin. But at its worst, incest fiction has the lifeless feel of a feminist textbook. "Let me tell you what it was *really* like," the writer seems to whisper in our ear, but so often that reality seems to be a stitched-together collection of political clichés. "I was like something he owned," writes Simpson. "You . . . felt . . . that fathers owned the bodies of their daughters," writes French. "We were just his, to do with as he pleased, like the pond or the houses or the hogs or the crops," writes Smiley. At moments like these, one hears the political wheels turning beneath the prose. French dedicates *Our Father* to Gloria Steinem, and we definitely feel Steinem picketing in her prose: "The only thing the four of them had in common was his . . . abuse. Maybe that was all women as a sex had in common." After reading these lines, the incest, no matter how dramatically described, appears to be simply an illustration of a political point.

This particular dark view of the family comes straight out of a literary tradition that began in the seventies with the profusion of men-are-bastards fiction; in the lively pages of well-loved

novels by writers like Hilma Wolitzer and Nora Ephron, husbands were always having affairs with their pregnant wives' best
friends.* Incest was the natural next step: men are not just bas-
tards; they're monsters.

As if the political predictability of these incest scenes is not
bad enough, there is also an astonishing sameness to the way they
are staged, even by writers with wildly different voices. Whether
they are narrated in the expressionless eighties deadpan of Simpson, Lewis, and Gaitskill, or with the tremulous anger of Atwood
and French, or the hallucinatory frenzy of King, the scenes themselves follow strikingly similar patterns. They are all rendered
with pornographic precision (none of the head-turning innuendo
of the incest in, say, F. Scott Fitzgerald's *Tender Is the Night*). We
see the act in cinematic detail—the penis, usually described as a
"hard thing," and the underwear, always described as "panties."
The drama itself is also recounted in remarkably similar terms:
"He pushed my skirt to the side and slid his left hand down between my legs," writes Allison. "He'd slide his hand . . . up my
leg, under my skirt," writes Banks. "He puts . . . his hands up
under her pleated school skirts and slides her panties right down,"
writes Atwood. Then come the obligatory fingers: "His fingers . . . gouging me," writes Gaitskill. "His fingers gouged at
me," writes Allison. "He was tearing my insides," writes French.

---

* Like Cheever and Updike, Salinger and Roth, these writers want to show the family's
hypocrisy, what happens behind locked doors, in bathrooms and bedrooms and base-
ments. But in choosing to do so in this particular way, they have created its mirror opposite, which is just as boring and implausible as the sitcoms of fifties domesticity. The
new incest novels have replaced one set of artificial characters with another: benign
patriarchs with brutal perverts.

"He was tearing me apart," writes Allison. And then there are the literal images of radical detachment: "My arms and legs flew from my pinned body to the corners of the ceiling, then back into their sockets, then back to the ceiling," writes Gaitskill. "She flies over to the window and in behind the curtain," writes Atwood.

By this point we anticipate the rhythms, the rubbing and touching in the lap scene, the father's smell, the escalation, the sneaking into bedrooms, the shame, the confusion, the disembodied child watching the scene from above. It all comes to sound the same—the stock plot of a culture obsessed with sexual abuse. What may once have been a daring subject, what astonished in Toni Morrison's *The Bluest Eye*, has now become paralyzed literary convention.*

There is, admittedly, no rule that writers have to write about new situations: we still want to read about love, adultery, and death. It wouldn't matter that the subject of incest is no longer fresh except that it so insistently announces its own freshness. When the writers of current incest novels darkly foreshadow what is to come, when they carefully build to the terrible scene, they rely on the shimmer and flash of novelty. They deliver the scene itself with the breathless tone of revelation: as each father

---

* The ancient taboo becomes simply a way to spice up sex scenes for a jaded reader. There is the vacant, stylish incest in Tartt's *The Secret History*. The fact that the tousled blond twins, Charles and Camilla, happen to be sleeping together lends no richness to the reader's understanding; it only contributes to the general ambience of bored decadence, like the martinis they drink and the pale garden party clothes they wear. The incest scene in Atwood's popular tale of female betrayal, *The Robber Bride*, may be more traumatic, but it is also entirely beside the point; vanishing into the general excesses of the abuse-filled story, it becomes as psychologically superfluous as the pink-icing flower on a birthday cake. It simply adds color.

slides under the covers with his young teenage daughter, the words themselves virtually quiver with the feeling, *I am the first person ever to have written about this.*

It's possible that the incest scene could be made new, but at this late date we can't help suspecting that the scene is the product of cultural opportunism, a sign that the author has lost sight of what separates literature from television drama. Beneath the swelling prose, the panties and the nightgowns, one feels the selling principle at work. Sex sells and perverse sex sells more— a sentiment confirmed during the fierce bidding war for Sapphire's *Push.* That the unfinished manuscript finally sold to Knopf for a reported $500,000 is testimony to the commercial potential of this particular form of suffering. Sapphire's novel itself is aptly named. The idea behind the larger literary trend toward sensationalism seems to be to push one step further, to push for the purest rage, the most lurid crime, the most innocent victim. The idea, finally, is to shock the virtually unshockable modern reader.

The irony is that while incest in life will never cease to appall us, incest in its written form is no longer shocking. After a while we read these scenes with the same numbness we feel watching people being blown up in the movies. Incest is no longer the dirtiest secret or the most unimaginable act, since we seem to talk about and imagine it all the time.

Young writers like Heather Lewis clearly have been reading their Dorothy Allison; Sapphire clearly has been reading her Alice Walker. And there is a whole new generation of writers, still in writing programs and dorm rooms, crumpling pages, drinking coffee, eyes fixed to their computers, who will read Lewis and Sapphire, as a new batch of novels with "dark secrets" and "harrowing pasts" finds its way onto editors' desks. Until one fine morning when some publisher gets out of bed and thinks, *I've heard enough about incest.* And some writer sits in her studio apartment typing away at her novel, thinking, *This is like nothing anyone has seen before.* And slowly at first, and then more quickly, other publishers and writers will turn, with good intentions, with dollar signs in their eyes, to the next hot subject, the next modish plot twist. Let it be soon.*

---

* In the years since I wrote this piece, there have been new vogues in fiction that work in much the same way: recently what comes to mind is "The —— Wife" genre, or the inside-the-mind-of-a-terrorist genre, or the amazing-mind-of-a-sensitive-child genre, along with the explosion of memoirs, many of which follow an arc of redemption and transcendence of the difficult or squalid past.

Joan Didion

1

Joan Didion devotees may be disappointed that *Where I Was From* is not, in spite of its title, a memoir. Or rather, it may be her version of a memoir—dazzling, theatrical, dense—but when it comes down to it, it is a book with very little of her life in it. The publishing materials refer to *Where I Was From* as "deeply and intensely personal," and yet what is striking is how impersonal the book actually is.*

Since the publication of *The White Album* and *Slouching*

---

*Didion's subsequent books, *The Year of Magical Thinking* and *Blue Nights*, both take up this same promise of memoir and confession. While they do in fact address her own experience more directly, they are both artful and elusive as well. One does not get a sense of what her relationship with either her husband or her daughter is like in either of these books, even though that would ostensibly be their subject. In many ways they are more intimate than her earlier books, but for memoirs, they still leave holes, pockets of deliberate vagueness, writerly lacunae. In both of these books she uses mood to tell her story, instead of more straightforward description, which allows her to evade certain direct information, or a less controlled or stylized characterization of the people in her life.

Towards Bethlehem, Didion has been celebrated as one of America's leading practitioners of a new kind of highly wrought personal journalism. In the *New York Observer,* Susan Faludi claimed that Didion taught a generation of writers how to make journalism "a personal expression." And Martin Amis characterized her style as "self-revealing" in an essay in which he went on to call her "a human being who managed to gouge another book out of herself rather than a writer who gets her living done on the side." But has her writing ever been that immediate, that personal, that raw? Has her confessional style ever been much more than just that—a style?

Didion seems at first glance to be revealing so much about herself because she makes great use of her mental fragility. Certain temperamental qualities of hers—her paranoia, her morbid sense of impending disaster, and her distrust of all stated realities—were particularly suited to the 1960s and '70s. Take the moment in *The White Album* when she writes about the "attack of nausea and vertigo" that led her to a psychiatric clinic. On the surface, this might seem like an intimate revelation about her inner life. And yet she ends the passage with "such an attack does not now seem to me an inappropriate response to the summer of 1968." This is typical Didion. It's as if her body were a finely tuned instrument for channeling the jittery mood of the country in flux. Her sense of doom, of highly calibrated alarm, is always in the service of some larger point; her stunned disbelief is always a commentary, on the times, on a murder, on the water supply, on Hawaii, on the bewildering state of California. It is never simply emotion for the sake of emotion. There is no pleasure in frankly exhibitionistic exposure; there is none of the blinkered narcissism of some of our more recent personal writing.

If there is a great deal of personality in her essays, there is very little that is personal. Even in her most superficially revealing essays, like her much-beloved "Goodbye to All That," autobiographical facts give way to typologies. Her crying in Chinese laundries becomes "what it's like to be young in New York." New York becomes "an infinitely romantic notion, the mysterious nexus of all love and money and power, the shining and perishable dream itself." In the end, for all the spare, vivid details about her walking down the street peering into the windows of brownstones, about drinking gazpacho when she is hungover, the essay is about moving to New York and about being young—not about Joan Didion moving to New York and being young. This is, in many ways, her gift: she leaves space for thousands of similarly disaffected readers to enter her prose and passionately identify with it.

Her stylistic tics add to the illusion of personal revelation. Didion frequently addresses the reader directly, as if we have entered an intimate form of conversation. She writes, "When John Wayne rode through my childhood, and perhaps through yours, he determined forever the shape of certain of our dreams." And her idiosyncratic cadences, her use of a kind of lulling, incantatory, biblical repetition, reinforces our sense of connection to her. Take this passage from *The White Album:* "It was Morrison who had described the Doors as 'erotic politicians.' It was Morrison who got arrested in Miami in December of 1967. . . . It was Morrison who got up there in his black vinyl pants with no underwear and projected the idea, and it was Morrison they were waiting for now."

And yet even after reading every single word Didion has ever published, how much does one know about her? One knows what

she packs on a trip to interview a subject, one knows about the
jasmine she smells on the way home from the airport in Los Angeles, but one knows almost nothing about her family, say, or her
marriage, or her daughter. The personal information she imparts
is so stylized, so mannered, so controlled, that it is no longer personal information.* The "I" in her essays is an elegant silhouette
of a woman. There is something shadowy about her, something
peculiarly obscure, like the famous photograph of her hiding behind huge sunglasses. She is, in the end, a writer of enormous
reserve.

Where I Was From covers some of the ordinary terrain of the
memoir; namely, it begins with her great-great-great-great-
great-grandmother's crossing the country in pioneer wagons and
ends with her mother's death. And in some way, she is writing
about her own reverse pioneering—her trip east, abandoning
everything she grew up with. But there is an evasion at the
center—a masterly, brilliant evasion but an evasion nonetheless.
In her riff on California, Didion examines, variously, Frank Nor-
ris, Jack London, the Spur Posse, the waterways, the Southern
Pacific Railroad, the paintings of Thomas Kinkade, the Bohemian Club, and the economy of the early nineties, and yet her
own relation to the place and to her family go largely unexamined. She teases out every contradiction, picks apart every myth,
and explodes every subtlety in mini critical essays, but when it
comes to her own background, she falls back on ordinary—if

---

* In the *Paris Review* interview with Didion, which came out after I wrote this piece, she
talked about her habit of retyping all of her work from the beginning every day (up to
a very high number of pages). This arduous work habit telegraphs how crafted her
writing is, how carefully wrought. It supports the view that the rawness people see in
her work is a carefully achieved effect, not a spontaneous outpouring of emotion.

perfectly crafted—description. Joan Didion, for all of her stylistic brio, becomes straightforward. She never gets beyond the cool surface. She is vague on certain crucial details. She writes, for instance, about her father going into a mental hospital for "some weeks or months." But she does not say why exactly or what she makes of it. Instead she goes on for several pages on the history of committing people to mental institutions in the state of California, suggesting that there is a shocking tradition of abandonment in that history, until one is finally dying to ask, What about her own father?

There is in her delicate, urban, neurotic sensibility something of the hardy pioneer ancestors she describes, jettisoning rosewood chests in the crossing, burying the dead on the wagon trail, never looking back. At one point she quotes another child of California, Patty Hearst, saying, "Never examine your feelings— they're no help at all."

So, why would she write a book that at least borders on being a memoir? *Where I Was From* is obsessed with unsatisfying graveyards: a family cemetery that was sold, children buried in trunks, women left in watery pools, or the dead buried on the trail, their graves run over with wagons. And in a way, this book represents another incomplete burial. Didion tells us the question "Where will I be from?" occurred to her when her mother died, and it seems that the impetus for this book came out of that death. One senses that Didion is attempting to bury her parents, and yet she doesn't quite. So much remains unsaid beneath the surface. Instead she writes what she always writes: about the lies we tell ourselves, about the absurdity of our desire for order, about the shamelessness and cowardice of human character. The usual elisions occur: she is writing about herself, she is writing about

California, she is writing about the founding myths. This is, like much in Didion, both frustrating and amazing. She is on some cool, understated, self-contained level channeling Walt Whitman, singing of America by singing of herself.

2

I don't think that I have ever walked into the home of a female writer, aspiring writer, newspaper reporter, or women's magazine editor and not found, somewhere on the shelves, a row of Joan Didion books. Very few women in the business have not, early in their careers, stayed up late into the night reading her, the sky streaked violet: "I could indulge here in a little idle generalization . . . could talk fast about convulsions in the society and alienation and anomie and maybe even assassination, but that would be just one more stylish shell game. I am not the society in microcosm. I am a thirty-four-year-old woman with long straight hair and an old bikini bathing suit and bad nerves sitting on an island in the middle of the Pacific waiting for a tidal wave that will not come." There it is. The brilliant paranoia. The sentences in love with their own drama.

On the cover of one of the books is a famous photograph of Didion, stick thin, hair blowing, brow furrowed, eyes hidden behind enormous black sunglasses, looking as if she needs a cigarette. She was the embodiment of everything cool in sixties journalism. Her writing was stylish, ironic, neurotic, and felt. Her sharp tone cut through the pretensions and weirdness of the times, but she also cried as she walked down the street and had migraine headaches and could barely get out of bed. That was her persona—bruised, fragile, harboring a mysterious sorrow that had something, but not everything, to do with the world around her. Didion wrote about murderers and fanatics and five-year-olds doing acid. She wrote, "I am so physically small, so temperamentally unobtrusive and so neurotically inarticulate that people tend to forget that my presence runs counter to their best interests." She did clipped irony and she did sentences swelling with portent. Hers was the quivering, sensitive sensibility of a generation, and still her words reverberate through our magazines and newspapers, her quirky, distinctive, oddly formal writing style borrowed and imitated, echoed and incorporated until it becomes simply the way we write. And it isn't a fleeting fashion. Nearly forty years after her first essays appeared in places like *The Saturday Evening Post,* we still imitate Joan Didion, and if we don't imitate Joan Didion, we imitate the people who imitate Joan Didion. Her rhythms are so mesmerizing, her insights so impressive, her personality so perversely appealing, that they lodge in the mind. It's no different from the boom of British authors writing like Martin Amis, or novelists drawing on Hemingway and Mailer, or painters drawing on Corot, but it is testimony to the power of Didion's style and the strength of her voice that it echoes into the casual pieces of this, the next century.

At the beginning of her classic collection of essays *The White Album* (1979), Didion quotes from her own psychiatric report and then says, "By way of comment I offer only that an attack of vertigo and nausea does not now seem to me an inappropriate response to the summer of 1968." That was one of the revelations of her style: the writer's own psyche became a delicate radio station channeling the outside world. The news was all about how the news makes you feel. And that is one of her most dubious legacies: she gave writers a way to write about their favorite topic (themselves) while seeming to pursue a more noble subject (the culture). It was a particular kind of cultural criticism she was pioneering, with childhood sleepovers and marital problems and tears folded delicately into the mix: navel-gazing with a social purpose. Didion did it elegantly, but many of those who followed did it not so elegantly.

Take Anna Quindlen and her endless chronicles of the world shrunk down into the television set in her living room, with her sons making Lego houses in the corner. If Didion developed a personal rapport with the reader, whom she speaks to directly in her essays as "you," Quindlen developed the kind of friendship with the reader where she sits at the kitchen table swapping recipes. Quindlen, who gained prominence on the op-ed page of *The New York Times* and then became a writer for *Newsweek*, was making her ideas palatable to the quintessential nineties audience, their bookshelves filled with memoirs and *Oprah* blaring from their television sets. In other words, an audience that wanted more intimacy and fewer ideas.

On one of the rare occasions when the outside world impinged on her interesting family life, at the end of the Persian Gulf War, Quindlen wrote: "Euphoria has been one of the war's buzzwords. We have been repeatedly cautioned not to feel it. The president said the other night this was not the time for it. It has never crossed my mind." The last sentence, the brisk personal reaction punctuating the public event, is pure Didion. The Gulf War also left Quindlen disoriented, she told us. "I am reasonably sure of only three things today," she wrote, "that George Bush will be re-elected president in 1992; that . . . he might win by the largest landslide in the history of the nation; and that we are incredibly skilled at war." This sense of being so stunned by the news that you can only be "reasonably sure" of a few things was one of Didion's most common states of mind. Didion herself put it this way: "I am talking here about a time when I began to doubt the premises of all of the stories I had ever told myself, a common condition but one I found troubling."

Of course, Quindlen is warmer, fuzzier, dopier, and more domestic than Didion, a tabby to Didion's panther. But there is a slightly hysterical strand running through Quindlen's extremely public breakfasts with her children that brings the older journalist to mind. You can hear a hint of Didion's emotional fragility, of that nausea and vertigo, for instance, in Quindlen's assertion that "I have never sat down to write about abortion without feeling, at least for a moment, the complexities sweep over me like a fit of faintness."

Quindlen was not the only *Times* writer to draw on Didion's sensibility. Remember when Maureen Dowd began to distinguish herself as a political reporter with her colorful ruminations on George Bush on the usually staid front page of *The New York Times?* Instead of simply reporting, Dowd took apart the news and analyzed it, breaking down the language of politics with quick sarcastic swipes. Like Didion, she proved herself a connoisseur of the small ironies and eccentric details of political hypocrisy. She observed. "But pork rinds, promoted by Mr. Atwater as a down-home staple of Mr. Bush's diet, have not been seen in the White House in nearly three years; Mr. Bush's favorite snack, it turns out, is popcorn." In her essays on people like John Wayne, or Huey Newton, or the Doors, or the Reagans, Didion wrote about what took place behind the image, about the intricate construction and manipulation of public perception. Take this memorable scene from an essay in which Didion writes about the then California governor's wife and a couple of photographers:

> "Nipping a bud," Nancy Reagan repeated, taking her place in front of the rhododendron bush.
>   "Let's have a dry run," the cameraman said.
>   The newsman looked at him. "In other words, by a dry run, you mean you want her to fake nipping the bud."
>   "Fake the nip, yeah," the cameraman said.

And then there's Dowd, in the front section of the *Times:*

> "Basic Parthenon shot?" the President asked the photographers who wanted to capture him standing in front of the ruins.

Dowd also imported into conventional newspaper articles Didion's habit of deeply scrutinizing people's choices of words. Dowd wrote, for instance. "At the Cabletron Systems computer parts plant in Rochester, he began a sentence concerning the Persian Gulf War with his usual manner of speaking, starting to say, 'about to begin,' and then thought better of it and switched to a Southern synonym mid-phrase. 'It was one year ago, one year ago that Desert Storm was about—fixin' to begin, as they say in another of my home states, Texas.'"

You can also hear Didion's cadences—as well as several of Didion's signature phrases—running beneath the political writing of Elizabeth Kolbert in *The New Yorker*. In a piece about the New York senatorial race, Kolbert writes: "In the months following, the fuss over 'Captain Jack' proved to be central to the emotional logic of Giuliani's election effort." Not only does the rhythm of the sentence echo Didion, but the "emotional logic" of an election effort is exactly the sort of thing Didion was constantly discussing. "Logic" also happens to be one of Didion's favorite words (Didion wrote: "As it happened I had always appreciated the logic of the Panther position" and "So many encounters in those years were devoid of any logic save that of dreamwork").

Things "appear" and "seem" in Joan Didion's writing. They are symbolic of and emblematic of; they characterize: they have morals and messages: they do not simply lie flat on the page. Which is also true of Kolbert: "The killing of Diallo, by contrast, seems to be emblematic of something new: a form of racial bias that is statistically driven and officially sanctioned and that, depending on your perspective, may or may not be racism at all." This sentence is also very Didion. She loves long, oddly constructed sentences, with ridiculously complicated syntax, often in the passive tense, that are weirdly beautiful, like tall and awkward teenagers. The artful and prolific use of the indirect phrase and the passive tense are aspects of Didion's signature style. Kolbert's phrase "may or may not be racism" is also pure Didion: a typographic illustration of ambiguity, as when Didion wrote, "The Getty's founder may or may not have had some such statement in mind."

And Kolbert also evokes Didion in her strategic use of quotation marks. Take the following Didionesque observations about stockbrokers: "Brokers routinely have days in which they are 'butchered' or 'killed' or 'annihilated' but dying on the floor is not regarded as an entirely metaphorical prospect." And "Last month, the First Couple completed their long-awaited move—

'move' here being understood in the loosest possible sense." This particular use of quotation marks is one of Didion's stylistic tics that have made their way so completely and thoroughly into our journalistic patois that they are almost hard to identify. Didion was so suspicious of received ideas that she filled pages with such observations as "The clothes were, as Mrs. Reagan seemed to construe it, 'wardrobe'—a production expense, like the housing and the catering and the first-class travel," or "To encourage Joan Baez to be 'political' is really only to encourage Joan Baez to continue 'feeling' things." Didion uses ironic, or what could be more accurately called skeptical, quotation marks fanatically and constantly. They highlight the fact that the journalist is not just telling a story, she is taking it apart; that the words we use are suspect, revelatory.

Travel writing also lends itself to Didion's dreamlike idiom. In the middle of her January 2000 piece in *The New Yorker* about Khao San Road in Bangkok, Susan Orlean interrupted her story to say: "I have a persistent fantasy that involves Khao San." Later, she writes, "From here you can embark on Welcome Travel's escorted tour of Chiang Mai . . . or an overland journey by open-bed pickup truck to Phnom Penh or Saigon, or a trip via some rough conveyance to India or Indonesia . . . or anywhere you can think of—or couldn't think of, probably, until you saw it named." Which brings to mind Didion's frequent trains of "or"s, such as "Music people never wanted ordinary drinks. They wanted sake, or champagne cocktails, or tequila neat. . . . We would have dinner at nine unless we had it at eleven-thirty, or we could order in later. . . . First we wanted a table for twelve . . . although there might be six more, or eight more."

So enduring and powerful is Didion's voice that her influence extends to writers who weren't even born when her first essays began to appear. Meghan Daum's 1999 essay in *The New Yorker* on leaving New York strongly evokes Joan Didion's famous reflection on the same subject, "Goodbye to All That," written thirty years earlier. Daum writes, "Once you're in this kind of debt—and by 'kind' I'm talking less about numbers than about my particular brand of debt—all those bills start not to matter anymore." Didion writes, "I do not mean 'love' in any colloquial way, I mean that I was in love with the city, the way you love the first person who ever touches you and never love anyone quite that way again."

Daum continues: "As it turned out, I did go to Vassar, and although it would be five years until I entered my debting era, my time there did more than expand my intellect." Didion uses the phrase "as it turned out" almost relentlessly in her writing, and she also loves to put complex temporal relations into a sentence in just that way. Here is Daum: "I'm kind of glad I didn't know, because I've had a very, very good time here. I'm just leaving the party before the cops break it up." Here is Didion: "It was a very long time indeed before I stopped believing in new faces and began to understand the lesson in that story, which was that it is distinctly possible to stay too long at the Fair."

Another young writer whose prose suggests late nights curled up with vintage Didion paperbacks is Sarah Kerr, writing here in *The New York Review of Books:* "But the arrangement did hold out a dream, a particularly Mexican parable of opportunity, for everyone in every sector, as a kind of glue." (Didion used the word "parable" over and over, as in "this is a California parable, but a true one" or "this may be a parable, either of my life as a reporter during this period or of the period itself," as well as

phrases like "particularly American" or "particularly Californ-
nian.")

"But that is to get ahead of the story," Kerr writes at one point
in her political analysis. Didion also assumed the role of the sto-
ryteller with lines like "I want to tell you a Sacramento story." In
fact, the idea of teasing out the "narratives" and "stories" and
"plots" of real life is one of Didion's trademarks. After the famous first line of her collection *The White Album,* "We tell ourselves stories in order to live," she might use the words "story" or
"narrative" up to fifteen or twenty times in a single essay. This
too has entered our journalistic conventions as a cliché. Here is
Lynn Darling in *Esquire:* "Marriage is for most of us the narrative
spine of our lives, the epic on which we hang our sense of who
we are." Here is Meghan Daum: "If there is in this story a single
moment when I crossed the boundary between debtlessness and
total financial mayhem, it's the first dollar that I put toward my
life as a writer in New York." And Elizabeth Kolbert: "The important story of his tenure is obviously the one about the city's
recovery." And it has become as commonplace for writers to reflect on their story, and the storylike nature of their story, and the
construction of The Story itself.

Didion's writing was so original, so distinctive, that paradoxically she has lost her originality. She has become mundane, traces
of her sharp personal lyricism scattered through newspapers and
magazines. One thinks here of Auden's elegy for Yeats: "he became his admirers." (There are also male writers who imitate
Didion, though more of them borrow from Tom Wolfe. Think
of all of those articles you've read in *GQ* and *Esquire* with such
Wolfian sound effects as "Splat!" and internal free associations
and liberal spatterings of exclamation points.)

But all of this influence could be the highest achievement a writer can hope for. It is Didion's incomparable style that seduces so many writers, but it is also the romantic persona she created: ambitious and vulnerable, narcissistic and paranoid and disoriented and maddeningly perceptive. The great revelation of her writing is that it was emotionally charged *and* coolly intellectual, after a journalistic tradition that was dry and distanced and straightforward.

One peculiar effect of Didion's absorption into the mainstream is that it has become hard to read her work without hearing the echoes. In her most recent novel, *The Last Thing He Wanted*, her fifth book since *The White Album*, she begins to sound like a parody of herself: "That she did not was the beginning of the story as some people in Miami came to see it."

Of course, one could argue that Didion herself may have been influenced by the women writers who came before her, by Mary McCarthy's essay "My Confession," about communism in the thirties, for example, or by Rebecca West's *The Meaning of Treason*, which took apart and channeled the experience of postwar England in the way Didion would later take apart and channel the experience of sixties America. But that, as Didion would say, is a whole other story.

Susan Sontag

1

If anyone is under the impression that Susan Sontag was just like everyone else, a quick perusal of *Reborn: Journals & Notebooks, 1947–1963*, edited by her son, David Rieff, should put that idea to rest. The extraordinary notebooks begin when she is a teenager, heading off to Berkeley, and carry her through her unhappy marriage to Philip Rieff, to Oxford and Paris, and, finally, back to New York. The diaries are shocking, singular, in both the intimacy of their brisk, notelike form and the astonishing personality they reveal.

Sontag does not expend the energy on being charming, or even comprehensible, that most people paradoxically do in their private journals. Her notes are scattered, aphoristic, sharp. There is a seriousness, an almost preternatural lack of humor, to the entries that is both the amazing power and the curiosity of Sontag's thought. The imperial voice of *Against Interpretation* is here aimed at herself. The critic takes her own personality on as a subject and dissects, often unflatteringly, her own weaknesses on the highest and most trivial levels. "I had never realized how bad my posture is," she writes. "It has always been that way. . . . It's not only that my shoulders + back are round, but that my head is thrust forward." The journals are largely composed of lists, ways to improve herself, books she should read, chronologies. They give evidence of a fierce and unrelenting campaign to work on herself as an intellectual, as a woman, as a mother. "In the journal," she writes, "I do not just express myself more openly than I could do to any person; I create myself." She was twenty-four years old.

What is remarkable here is the ferocious will, the conscious and almost unnatural assembly of a persona that rises above and beyond that of ordinary people. The determination she devotes to figuring out who to be, on the most basic and most sophisticated levels, is breathtaking. "Better to know the names of flowers than to confess girlishly that I am ignorant of nature," Sontag writes. There is, in these pages, no sense of a woman comfortable in the world, a woman at ease. "Don't smile so much, sit up straight," she admonishes. "Think about why I bite my nails in the movies." How is it possible that anyone is this self-conscious? And how is it possible that this degree of self-consciousness could be so fruitful?

In fact, there is no other diary I can think of that makes such liberal use of the imperative mood. Sontag is unremitting in her efforts to transcend her limitations, to imagine a different way of existing. She writes, "Admitting my mistakes, when I have been cheated or taken advantage of—a luxury that should be rarely indulged. People may seem to sympathize, really they despise you a little. Weakness is a contagion, strong people rightly shun the weak." She seems to harbor a secret image of herself as sloppy, idle, and weak that lies somewhere behind her spectacular efforts; she writes of herself over and over as naturally weak and accommodating to other people. The strength we associate with Sontag is an image, it seems, that she labored on, like an essay. In these strange and admirable journals, she feels at times like an alien from another planet who has settled in our midst and is studying our ways: "Most Americans start making love as if they were jumping out a window with their eyes closed." One can't help coming away with a sense of one's own slack acceptance of a comfortable existence.

In the passages about her romantic life, which are the most conventionally human in the journals, Sontag comes across as surprisingly ardent and vulnerable. By her own account, she has a series of relationships with women in which she loves more than she is loved. "H. thinks she is decadent because she has entered into a relationship which neither physically or emotionally interests her. How decadent then am I, who know how she really feels and still want her?" All of the confidence we associate with Sontag, the opinionated force of her personality, crumbles in these associations with women in a manner almost hard to watch. Her descriptions of her affairs are filled with pain and self-contempt: "I can already envisage H.'s brittle demonstrativeness, my own gaucherie—my idiotic attempts to elicit her love."

The Sontag in these diaries is mesmerizing, brilliant, abrasive, not quite likeable. Rieff mentions that he has not edited extensively and that she never read her journals out loud or intended for other people to read them. This appears to be true. They feel raw, unprocessed, like scribbled notes to herself, which gives them a greater power and immediacy than other, more polished diaries and memoirs that seem to anticipate and cater to their public. They were meant for *her*, and she did not write and move on: Sontag comments in the margins later, like a professor weighing in judgment on a former self, never leaving herself alone. There is in an important way no difference between her own experience and a particularly absorbing book she might be reading. One can't help but admire the intricate mental apparatus at work: she is writing notes on her notes. These private jottings are, like her famous essays, almost entirely abstract and cerebral: she almost never describes the physical world, what the sky looked like, the smell of orange trees in Seville, or what she and her lover ate for breakfast.

And yet the innumerable tiny details that preoccupy Sontag over the years, the moments when she does describe her relation to the physical world, are revealing. There are a surprising number of entries in which she resolves to bathe more frequently. "Take a bath every day," she writes over and over, which somehow one doesn't imagine reading in the journals of an adult. But bathing is difficult for her; it involves a confrontation with the physical body she finds distressing. She tells us she sometimes falls asleep in her clothes. There is something endearing in this self-portrait: the arrogant command of her authorial voice somehow belied by a sweet image of the unworldly woman writer, so uncomfortable with the basic physical demands of life, so flustered by soap and water.

If there was any doubt, the notebooks confirm that the uncompromising intelligence, the unsparing honesty Sontag shows in her work is not a pose or affectation. Her entries give evidence that she is to her core as unrelenting, unironic a critic in life as she is in her work. The harshness and purity and impossibility of her writing carry through into her days. All the weakness she fears in

herself, the baroque and excessive self-contempt she feels, is mar-
shaled for the highest cause: she wills herself into a strength of
vision and ambition of voice unrivaled in a woman thinker. She
writes, "The writer is in love with himself," and so she labors to
create a self she can love, to reflect that perfect, arrogant writer's
confidence, that necessary narcissism. In his rather beautiful and
tormented introduction, Rieff wonders whether he should have
published these journals at all, as his mother never made her
wishes clear before she died. But the reader, at least, is grateful
that he did. The notebooks are invaluable for anyone interested
in how the serious and flamboyant intellectual dreamed up her
greatest project: herself.

2

One can't say Susan Sontag died a particularly private death. She
once declared she wouldn't tell her readers "what it is really like
to emigrate to the kingdom of the ill and live there," but it seems
other people were determined to do it for her. The latest glimpse
we have of her sickbed is *Swimming in a Sea of Death*, David
Rieff's superbly intelligent, disordered account of his mother's
final illness.

It is perhaps not surprising that Rieff objects violently to the
frank and controversial photographs that Annie Leibovitz took
of his mother as she was dying. He writes that Sontag was "hu-
miliated posthumously" by Leibovitz's "carnival images of celebrity death."

Rieff himself seems to have made a compromise with the
business of intimate revelation; in his indirection one feels the

tastefulness, the reserve, of the reluctant or ambivalent memoir-
ist. His images of his mother are vague, a figure weeping in another room; if they were sketches, they would be rendered in a
delicate charcoal smudge. We see her underlining a pamphlet put
out by the Leukemia and Lymphoma Society, but we do not see
her illness itself in any detail. Rieff tells us he is not taking notes
during her final months (which echoes Leibovitz's assertion that
she stopped taking pictures during that same time). He tells us, in
one elliptical passage, that "she might be covered in sores, incon-
tinent and half delirious," but he does not want to write straightforwardly that she is.

What is shocking about the memoir is how ordinary Sontag
seems. The reactions of this strong, singular woman to her illness, as Rieff reports them, are oddly generic. In a car returning
from receiving the terrible diagnosis, he writes, she looks out the
window, and " 'Wow,' she said, 'Wow.' " It tells us something important, surely, that one of the most articulate women of the last
century should say, in the face of her cancer, "Wow."

In fact, Sontag's confrontation with her own ordinariness is
the most intriguing element of Rieff's story. For a woman who
had always believed in her own exceptionality, who had defined
herself by her will to be different, to rise above, the terrifying
democracy of illness is one of its most painful aspects. Throughout her final illness, she tells Rieff, "This time, for the first time in
my life, I don't feel special." In the most profound and affecting
passages of the book, Rieff questions whether, on some level, his
mother thought that she was too special to die. He investigates
the line between hubris and bravery, grandiosity and vitality. Do
we ever truly accept that we will die? Is there a part of the mind,
especially for someone as ambitious, as avid, as Sontag, that re-

fuses to believe in its own extinction? Rieff enumerates the qualities that enabled her to transcend her unhappy girlhood in Arizona and her early unhappy marriage to become one of the country's most formidable intellectuals. "Her sense that whatever she could will in life she could probably accomplish . . . had served her so well for so long that, empirically, it would have been madness on her part not to have made it her organizing principle, her true north," he writes. That same belief in the power of her own desire, that spectacular ambition, that intellectual bravado, made it impossible to accept that fatal illness was not another circumstance she could master.

Of course, Sontag's belief in her exceptionality had a history. In her first bout with breast cancer in her early forties, she survived. In early interviews after her recovery, she seemed intoxicated by her brush with death. She claimed she had acquired a "fierce intensity" that she would bring to her work; and she incorporated the idea of radical illness into the drama of her intellect, the dark glamour of her writer's pose. Sontag had written in her diary during her treatment that she needed to learn "how to turn it into a liberation." And it was that determination, that stubbornness, that constant act of self-transcendence that she thought she could reproduce at seventy-one, when cancer was diagnosed for a third time. But this time it didn't work. "She had the death that somewhere she must have come to believe that other people had from cancer," Rieff writes, "the death where knowledge meant nothing, the will to fight meant nothing, the skill of the doctors meant nothing."

For a writer who voluntarily embarks on a memoir about his mother, Rieff is curiously silent on the subject of their relationship, but the contrast in styles speaks for itself. If Sontag was incomparable in her confidence, grand scale in her ambition, constitutionally incapable of self-irony, her son is the opposite. He is disarming in his tentativeness, his self-doubt. "I am not even remotely smart enough to resolve any of this, even in my own mind," he writes.

The book is haunted by Rieff's anxiety that Sontag may have undergone an arduous treatment that was almost certain to fail, and in doing so put herself through an unnecessary ordeal. One of the doctors Rieff consults suggests a "folie à deux" between some cancer patients and their doctors, where physicians offer elaborate treatments, holding out hope when there is essentially none, in order to honor their patients' last wishes to battle their disease. Did Sontag undergo a painful and doomed bone marrow transplant because she refused to accept the basic medical facts of her case? Rieff suggests that she might have. She struggled past the moment it was rational to struggle. Rieff seems to wish she had died a more peaceful death.

One of the fascinations of this memoir is watching Sontag's thoughts play themselves out in the medium of life. In her elegant polemic *Illness as Metaphor,* she argues against the various fantasies that surround disease. Instead of poetry and emotionally charged beliefs, she argues, patients need to see clearly, think rationally, arm themselves with medical information to prepare themselves for the hard work of the cure. When Sontag was sick, she wrote in her journals that "I have become afraid of my own imagination." It was this fear she so brilliantly investigated and rejected in *Illness as Metaphor.* The imagination, the romantic overlay we give disease, becomes the patient's worst enemy.

The purity and charisma of the ideas Sontag laid out in *Illness as Metaphor* are irresistible, and yet this time around, for Sontag, seeing clearly and absorbing information would lead only to the certain knowledge that she would die. In her final confrontation with cancer, she needed consolation; she needed fantasy; she needed not to think clearly. This was the dilemma for Rieff: Should he act according to what he felt his mother wanted as she lay in her hospital bed, nurturing false hopes and offering comforting lies? Or should he follow the dictates of her rigorous, uncompromising work, and tell her the truth? Rieff returns again and again to his guilt over whether he should have been more honest. The book's very structure mimics the restlessness of a family member in a hospital room: pacing, circling, hovering. In the end, Sontag couldn't live her illness without metaphor; she needed the idea of a fight even after the fight was lost.

Ultimately, Sontag's strength is hard to disconnect from her folly. Her way of dying seems impossible, arrogant, heroic. Her conclusions, so hard won, so beautifully wrought, in *Illness as Metaphor*, seem a luxury here. In the introduction to that book, Sontag wrote about the kingdom of the ill, but in the real kingdom of the ill, as Rieff reminds us, there is no place to ruminate on metaphors: there is only death. From her bed at Memorial Sloan-Kettering, when she was recovering from breast cancer, Sontag wrote in her journal, "In the valley of sorrow, spread your wings." Rieff, his mother's son, unwilling to mystify, to romanticize, adds that "this was not the way she died." But it is, of course, the way she lived.

The Ambiguities of Austen

Back in 1905, Henry James complained about "the body of publishers, editors, illustrators, producers of magazines, which have found their dear, our dear, everybody's dear Jane so infinitely to their material purpose." Imagine how James would feel today were he to witness the blossoming commercial manifestations of our current Jane Austen craze. Over the past few years, Austen's quiet courtship novels have been made into Hollywood movies, analyzed by fashionable male writers like Martin Amis, and displayed above front counters of Barnes & Nobles across the country.

Though she has long been a staple of high school English classes, our recent affection for this writer born over two centuries ago has less to do with the transcendent literary merit of her novels than with what she has come to represent. In the midst of our contemporary confusion about gender roles and sexuality, Jane Austen has come to symbolize clarity and order. In a world in which millions of women buy books like *The Rules* or *He's Just Not That into You* in order to gain insight into their romantic lives, where the majority of babies born to women under thirty are born to single mothers, *Pride and Prejudice* promises a few hours of calm and certainty. Jane Austen is best loved for the lost romantic world she describes, for the bright green lawns of a distant English countryside, where the virtue of marriage was a truth universally acknowledged, and love was formal, restrained, and inevitable.

Most of us are intimately acquainted with Emma Woodhouse, Elizabeth Bennet, and the Dashwood sisters, but we tend to know very little about their creator. Jane Austen lived as a spinster in what is tactfully referred to by her biographers as "genteel poverty." Her books were published anonymously—"By a lady"—because it was considered inappropriate for a woman of her class to write novels. And though they did achieve a certain amount of critical success and notoriety during her lifetime, it was not until after her death that they became immensely popular. Austen lived her whole life dependent on relatives and plagued by financial worries, and she died of what was most likely Addison's disease at forty-one.

There is a certain amount of irony to the title of the new biography—*Jane Austen: Obstinate Heart* tells us almost nothing about the author's heart, obstinate or otherwise. It's the kind of biography that casts aside troublesome questions of psychology and motivation for the more tangible details of roast-beef dinners, yearly incomes, and lace-trimmed cloaks. Valerie Grosvenor Myer offers a responsible, if plodding, account of the minutiae of Austen's daily life while studiously ignoring issues of potentially greater interest—like how she felt about her romantic involvements or her art.

To be fair to the biographer, the information we have about Jane Austen's inner life is somewhat limited. Her family destroyed crucial passages from her letters, including an intriguing one she wrote on her deathbed about her "domestic disappointment." As a result, any portrait of Jane Austen is necessarily sketchy and speculative. As Myer points out, we don't even know with any certainty what the author looked like. With conflicting accounts of her appearance and no authenticated professional portrait, we can only piece together her features like police artists making a composite sketch of a criminal.

The Jane Austen who emerges from the pages of this new biography is cranky and unpleasant. Myer is so eager to discredit the already much discredited myth of Jane Austen's sugar-sweet femininity that she bends too far in the opposite direction: she dwells almost entirely on what she admiringly refers to as the novelist's "vinegary" side. The reader may be alerted to this not-entirely-balanced view of Austen's character by the biographer's assertion, in the very first paragraph of the book, that her subject looks in one drawing like "a peevish hamster."

The greatest flaw in *Obstinate Heart*, however, is that the biographer largely neglects what is probably the richest evidence of Jane Austen's inner life: the novels themselves. Readers seeking a more satisfying account of the novelist's life and how she processed her life into art should read Park Honan's lively and passionate *Jane Austen: Her Life.*

In spite of what Honan calls her subject's "comic violence," her gift for social satire, her ability to cut down her characters in a single sentence, Jane Austen was also the master of the happy ending—the implausible, heartwarming happy ending. Vladimir Nabokov called *Mansfield Park*, which he greatly admired, a "fairy tale," and in some sense all of her novels are fairy tales.

None of Jane Austen's heroines is disappointed in love. None of them ends up with a man of less than perfect character, with less than a large estate and income, or a gracious country parish.

But it is precisely this type of happy ending that eluded the author in her own life. She dreamed up Emma and Mr. Knightley's flirtatious banter, Elizabeth Bennet and Mr. Darcy's electricity, and Anne Elliot and Captain Wentworth's constancy, but she herself remained alone. And it is the contrast between her fantasies and her days, her fiction and her life, that is the central mystery of any biographical study of Jane Austen: Why did the author of our quintessential marriage plots herself never get married?

As a young girl, Jane Austen was interested enough in marriage to make imaginary entries for herself and a fictional husband in her father's parish register. With her auburn curls and bright brown eyes, she was by almost all accounts attractive. She never fit the stereotype of the shy, reclusive female writer who shuts herself off from human company, and instead loved dances, clothes, and flirtations. In fact, one gossip actually referred to one of the century's most brilliant novelists as "the prettiest, silliest, most-affected, husband-hunting butterfly."

It appears that she did have a few romances, or what passed for romances in that more restrained era—a shadowy man she met by the seaside who died, an Irishman who ran away because of her lack of money, another who bought her a present of silk stockings, a reverend, and a wealthy landowner with a stutter. But she never ended up attaching herself to anyone. She often responded to the rise and fall of romantic expectations with the lightness and humor that would later enter the tone of her novels.

She wrote to her sister Cassandra about one of her suitors, "I rather expect to receive an offer. But I will refuse unless he promises to give away his white coat."

In this age of transgressive biographical speculation, the predictable rumors that Jane Austen was a lesbian made their way from the quiet pages of the *London Review of Books* to a glossy item in *Newsweek* several years ago. But that is far too convenient an explanation of Jane Austen's psyche. In one of her rare attempts at psychological insight, Myer writes that "despite her youthful popularity, all Jane's relationships with men came to nothing. Her obstinate heart forbade her to marry except for love." But the question remains: Why *didn't* she fall in love? The answer may be a combination of pennilessness and bad luck, but it may also be more emotionally complicated. It may be that Jane Austen, the author of the nineteenth century's greatest tributes to married happiness, herself had deeply ambivalent feelings about the institution.

In the imaginative universe of her novels, marriage is the ultimate goal toward which all of her independent, spirited heroines are pulled as if by a natural force like gravity. Although she mocks Mrs. Bennet's eagerness to marry off her daughters in *Pride and Prejudice,* the author herself seems equally eager to marry off the Bennet girls.

But it turns out, if you read her letters, that Jane Austen had quite a different attitude when it came to real life. She writes to her favorite niece, Fanny Knight, "Oh, what a loss it will be when you are married! You are far too agreeable in your single state— too agreeable as a niece. I shall hate you when your delicious play of mind is all settled down into conjugal and maternal affections." This playful lament betrays larger concerns about what

THE AMBIGUITIES OF AUSTEN

marriage actually entails; it may be that Austen was worried about her own "delicious play of mind" and the terrible toll that marriage and childbirth take on the independent spirit.

Though it seems like a feminist cliché conjured up by a professor at a conference, Jane Austen really did seem to respond to the realities of nineteenth-century married life with something very much like horror. She watched the women around her have eleven, twelve, and thirteen children and give up their entire lives to the process of childbearing. She also saw four of her sisters-in-law die during or shortly after childbirth. "Poor animal," she writes of her vibrant niece Anna on learning that she is pregnant, "she will be worn out before she is thirty." It is also telling that Jane Austen referred to her novels repeatedly as "my own darling child" or "my suckling," and it may be that in her own mind she exchanged maternity for creativity, children for novels.

Austen's ambivalence toward marriage reveals itself in her more obscure novellas and in the subplots of her major works. She attaches a kind of glamour to the women who manage to elude, even for a while, the traditional marriage plots that dominate most of her books. Her memorable flirts, like the manipulative Mary Crawford in *Mansfield Park* and the protagonist of her little-read novella *Lady Susan*, live outside of the conventional domestic order. "I cannot easily resolve on anything so serious as marriage," writes the formidable Lady Susan, "especially as I am not at present in want of money."

Both Lady Susan and Mary Crawford are portrayed as villainesses, but their freedom to float above the rest of the characters, their independence, their ability to control their own lives and manipulate reality, are described with a certain relish and fascination. Lady Susan is "clever and agreeable, has all that knowledge of the world that makes conversation easy, and talks very well with a happy command of language, which is too often used, I believe, to make black appear white." Jane Austen's coquettes are powerful. They invent their own lives in ways that the Emmas and Elinors and Fannys never can, and in that sense they may perhaps be more of a reflection of the author herself.

There are two Jane Austens—the Jane Austen who glorifies domestic order and the Jane Austen who struggles against it. Though we tend to look at her novels nostalgically, as pretty dreams of order and harmony in our own world of chaos and loneliness, they seemed in fact to serve the same psychological function for the author herself. Beneath the idealized romantic universe she sets down with her ivory quill pen are the same yearning and ambivalence as those of her present-day reader. It is the tension between fantasy and life, between the desire for happy endings and the suspicion of happy endings, between conventionality and a deep uneasiness with conventionality, that marks Jane Austen as a truly modern writer and accounts for the continuing power and immediacy of her novels, and the enduring fascination with her world.

Rabbit at Rest

Three years after his death, it's sad to see that John Updike has subtly fallen out of fashion, that he is left off best-novels lists like the Modern Library's, and that a faint sense of disapproval clings to his reputation, even as his immense talent is recognized.

In fact, his immense talent is part of what people seemed to find suspect about him in the years before his death. Critics and writers seem to hold the fact that he writes beautiful sentences against him, as if his writing is too well crafted, too flamboyantly, extravagantly good. James Wood wrote a decade ago, "He is a prose writer of great beauty, but that prose confronts one with the question of whether beauty is enough, and whether beauty always conveys what a novelist must convey." Here, of course, one has to wonder about that special handbook of "What a Novelist Must Convey," and the rules and regulations contained therein.

And yet many other writers over the years have harbored the same odd objection. Take this critique in *The New Republic:* his "sheer verbal power, the cormorant-like ingestion of experience and its seemingly effortless conversion into 'brilliant' language isn't itself sufficient for great fiction. It may even in some ways be inimical to it." Or this one in *Commentary:* "He simply can't pass up any opportunity to tap dance in prose." The idea is that we should somehow distrust Updike because he is too good a writer. The word "stylish" in this way of thinking becomes a slur, as does the word "beautiful."

The faux-democratic ideal of plainspokenness, the sense that a novelist should not write too beautifully or he will sacrifice some vaguely articulated, semi-mystical claim to honesty, is not a million miles away from the Sarah Palin–ish suspicion of East Coast liberals, or a Harvard education, or people who know the dates of wars. This is not to say that writing beautifully or elaborately is *necessary* for good fiction, but that one can't deny that there are writers (Henry James, Nabokov, Flaubert) who write beautiful or elaborate sentences without any sacrifice to some mysterious, indefinable fictional mission.

In an interview with the *New York Times*'s Sam Tanenhaus a couple of months before his death, Updike addressed this cluster of issues in his own gracious way: "I don't really think of myself as writing stylishly. I think of myself as trying to write with precision about what my mind's eye conjures up." Of course, his critics might object to even this phrasing as perhaps a little fancy. Why can't John Updike speak in plain English? But it is exactly the poetic precision in his writing that his critics seem to find so unnerving.

Updike has also been repeatedly attacked for "misogyny," for two-dimensional women, for mistreating his lady characters. (Frederick Crews complains that Updike's male characters are "routinely unfaithful, maddeningly indecisive and self-absorbed"; David Foster Wallace calls them "incorrigibly narcissistic, philandering, self-contemptuous and self-pitying . . . they never really love anybody.") These characters are not, in this view, very lovely to their wives and girlfriends. But even if this is true, and it's arguably not the full and nuanced truth, this has always seemed to me a strange objection, as great novels from *Crime and Punishment* to *Lolita* to *Wings of the Dove* often delve into the consciousness of someone not quite savory. In fact, novels portraying the minds of totally fair-minded, upstanding, liberal people with very few conflicts about conventional life, who treat everyone around them extremely nicely, seem destined or at least highly likely to be sort of blah.

The writer's obligation, surely, is to write a charismatic, interesting, illuminating novel about, really, anyone. But this idea that Updike has the responsibilities of a senator, or school principal, or pastor toward his fictional universe, an obligation for fairness and justice to all of his characters, for a clear-sighted, unwavering morality that extends over his New England and Pennsylvania towns, and even according to a surprising number of critical briefs against him, for well-rounded theological positions, perversely endures.

Updike offers his own engaging mea culpa about his relation to women in a poem: "I drank up women's tears and spat them out / as 10-point Janson, Roman, and *Ital.*" This seems, however, more of an indictment of the way writers treat other people, male and female, than a confession of his sexist attitudes. Do writers use and arguably exploit those around them? Of course. Is there something unappealing or ruthless about this way of existing in the world? Of course, again. But this is not a commentary on Updike and his uses of female experience so much as a description of the writer's life (see female writers like Sylvia

Plath or Mary McCarthy), and if Updike addresses this moral dubiousness honestly and head-on that should be to his credit.

From the beginning, Updike wrote about trying to defeat death or mortality through affairs, through the intensity of sex, which is one of the things David Foster Wallace in particular criticizes him for. Updike describes an affair in *Toward the End of Time*: "Its colorful weave of carnal revelation and intoxicating risk and craven guilt eclipsed the devouring gray sensation of time."

This sense of using sex, or the creation of many lives, through affairs, and mistresses, transcending the limits of one small, suburban existence through sex, runs through Updike's writing from the beginning. In one story he has an amazing description of a man running into a former mistress: "I felt in her presence the fear of death a man feels with a woman who once opened herself to him and is available no more."

And so it is as someone who has always resisted, written around, plotted against, and fought the idea of death that he writes movingly about its proximity in his last book, a remarkable collection of poems, *Endpoint*.

The poems, which he wrote as he was dying, have an alarming clarity to them, a cool descriptiveness. He is still interested in the ironies, still interested in the celebration and the blooming style. He wrote the following a month before he died about a CAT scan and needle biopsy, and the pleasant clouding of Valium:

I heard machines and experts murmuring about me—
A dulcet tube in which I lay secure and warm
And thought creative thoughts, intensely so,
As in my fading prime. Plans flowered, dreams.

All would be well, I felt, all manner of thing.
The needle, carefully worked, was in me, beyond pain,
Aimed at the adrenal gland. I had not hoped
to find, in this bright place, so solvent a peace.
Days later, the results came casually through:
The gland, biopsied, showed metastasis.

In another one of his last poems he wrote, "be with me, words, a little longer." And after three years in an Updike-less world, one wishes the same thing.

Do Childish People Write Better Children's Books?

For all the years that I had been reading *Goodnight Moon* to some child or other, I had been picturing its author as a plump, maternal presence, someone like the quiet old lady in the rocking chair whispering "Hush," and so I was surprised to see, in a bored, casual dip into Google, the blond, green-eyed, movie-starish vixen, and attendant accounts of her lesbian lover, her many male lovers, her failure to settle down, and her tragic early death.

Margaret Wise Brown, or "Brownie" as her friends called her, did not harbor sentimental notions and was not overly devoted to bunnies and chubby toddlers. In a *Life* profile the reporter expressed surprise that the tender creator of so many rabbit-themed books would enjoy hunting and shooting rabbits, and Margaret replied, "Well, I don't especially like children, either. At least not as a group. I won't let anybody get away with anything just because he is little."

One of Margaret Wise Brown's offhand descriptions of childhood makes me think that she was nearer to childhood than the rest of us, inside it in a way that most of us can't quite imagine or get to: she talks about the "painful shy animal dignity with which a child stretches to conform to a strange, adult social politeness." Could there be a better, more intimate expression of that awkward childhood relation to the adult world?

Also preternaturally incisive about that stage of life is her statement about the purpose of kids' books: "to jog him with the unexpected and comfort him with the familiar." Putting both the jogging and the comforting together is too resplendent an insight for an expert on childhood and seems to belong instead to a denizen of it.

Is it possible that the most inspired children's book writers never grow up? By that I don't mean that they understand or have special affection or affinity toward children, but that they don't understand adulthood, and I mean that in the best possible sense. It may be that they haven't moved responsibly out of childhood the way most of us have, into busy, functional, settled adult life.

Margaret Wise Brown's life was full of what her admirers like to call whimsy and other people might call childlike behavior. She spent her first royalty check on an entire cart full of flowers. At her house in Maine, which she called "The Only House," she had an outdoor boudoir with a table and nightstand and a mirror nailed to a tree, along with an outside well that held butter and eggs, and wine bottles kept cold in a stream; one could easily imagine a little fur family living in The Only House, but it was just her friends, associates, editors, and lovers passing through. She was once chastised by a hotel owner in Paris because she had brought giant orange trees and live birds into her room. The orange trees might have been okay, but the live birds were a little de trop.

It also seems that she could be annoying in the way only an

energetic seven-year-old could be: a friend asks her the time, and she says, "What time would you like it to be?" She had a group called the Bird Brain Society, in which the members could declare any day Christmas and the rest would come over and celebrate it. She was, in other words, one of those people whose magnetism owes something to the fact that the line between play and life is never entirely clear to them.

Virginia Woolf captures this quality in her description of Lewis Carroll: "For some reason, we know not what, his childhood was sharply severed. It lodged in him whole and entire. He could not disperse it." Lewis Carroll, a stuttering lifelong bachelor who preferred playing games with children for hours to adult company, was not alone in this respect. Maurice Sendak's unhappy childhood always seemed bitterly, creatively alive in him, though he had a very happy long-term relationship with a psychiatrist, Eugene. "I refuse to lie to children," Sendak once said. "I refuse to cater to the bullshit of innocence." And like Margaret Wise Brown, Kay Thompson, the author of the Eloise books, an actress, a film star, and a nightclub singer, apparently led a racy, interesting, unsettled life, and said to those inquiring about who the little girl was based on: "Eloise is me! All me."

For Margaret Wise Brown, underneath all of this whimsicality or childlike behavior there was, of course, some isolation and turmoil. Her relationship with her lesbian lover, Michael Strange, whom she privately, and perhaps not surprisingly, called Rabbit, was rocky and tormented. Michael once took an illustrator aside and said, "Why don't you marry Margaret and take her off my hands?" Margaret never had children of her own, and her affairs were often unstable. The playful, ebullient social presence obscured periods of despair and loneliness.

But anyway, just something to think about as you are reading "In the great green room there was a telephone and a red balloon. . . ." The great soothing anthem of millions of American childhoods was conjured by someone restless, unsettled. Maybe it makes sense that the great dream or poem of domestic peace should come from someone for whom that peace is charged, elusive.

Margaret Wise Brown died tragically early at forty-two, though it should be noted that she died playfully. She was in France, hospitalized for appendicitis ("I've really enjoyed this odd French Hospital," she wrote to a friend), and after the routine operation she seemed to be recovering uneventfully. One morning she kicked her leg can-can style to show a nurse how well she was, and an embolism killed her instantly.

At the time Margaret was about to be married to her much younger fiancé, "Pebbles" Rockefeller. She was touring France, and he was sailing to meet her on his boat. It's possible that she was just then on the verge of growing up or settling down or becoming more ordinary. Though one half imagines Pebbles Rockefeller sailing somewhere, and Margaret saying, "If you become a sailboat and sail away from me, I will become the wind and blow you where I want you to go."

PART III

The Way We Live Now

The Perverse Allure
of Messy Lives

One day an editor asked me to write about the enormous popularity of the television show *Mad Men*. I was entirely willing to do so, except for one small obstacle, which is that I had never watched a single episode. I spent several days watching so much of the show that I almost felt like I should write my article in front of a manual typewriter in a pencil skirt.

I could see why people were transfixed by the pouring of cocktails in the office, by the lighting of cigarettes with silver lighters, by the extramarital carousing of advertising executives in hats. The phenomenal success of the show seemed to rely at least in part on the thrill of casual vice, on the glamour of spectacularly messy, self-destructive behavior to our relatively staid and enlightened times. In some larger cultural way, we have moved in the direction of the gym, of the enriching, wholesome pursuit, of the embrace of responsibility, of the furthering of goals, and away from lounging around in the middle of the afternoon with a drink.

The show derives its particular electricity from the differences, from the moments that contrast sharply with the way we live now. As one watches the feverish and melancholic adultery, the pregnant women sipping cocktails, the seven-year-olds learning to mix the perfect Tom Collins, one can't help but experience a puritanical frisson about how much better, saner, more sensible our own lives are; but is there also the tiniest bit of wistfulness, the slight but unmistakable hint of longing toward all that stylish chaos, all that selfish, retrograde abandon? The fascination is not unmixed. If the characters in *Mad Men* are smoldering against the famous repression of the fifties, it may be that we smolder a little against the wilier and subtler repression of our own undoubtedly healthier, more upstanding times.

Which is to say that these days, the careful anthropologist observes brief furtive forays into the world of excess in highly functional and orderly people. I notice more than one mother sneaking out of a party for a secret cigarette in my garden; I hear another talk about how she has two or three glasses of wine every night, how she might be an alcoholic, and yet another describe a Facebook flirtation with someone from her past. One hears the faint murmur of these guilty pleasures, these tiny rebellions, these harmless, momentary flares of intensity or escape, and yet, in the end these vices are so minor and controlled. The large-scale messiness of *Mad Men* is not for these modest rebels, the free fall into chaos, into a stranger's warm and enticing bed; it frightens and enthralls them. What they want, in other words, is to watch four seasons of it through the safe, skewed mirror of the television set.

In my casual investigation into those lost years, I have lunch with Jerry Della Femina, whose 1970 cult classic memoir, *From Those Wonderful Folks Who Gave You Pearl Harbor*, is widely considered the inspiration for *Mad Men*. I notice that when he talks about those days in the advertising business he uses the word "fun," which stands out to me suddenly as exotic and old-fashioned. Who has fun in the office anymore? Maybe we are disappearing into Facebook or email or foreign newspapers or shopping, but we are not expecting the flagrant flirtation or cocktail party atmosphere of Sterling Cooper; we are not expecting what Jerry Della Femina means by "fun."

These days, people of Don Draper's age and situation pour energy into beautiful vacations, or cook lemon ricotta capellinis and salmon crème fraiche risottos from organic free-range ingredients for a dinner party. But are they hanging out with the same boozy fluidity, are there wild bursts of bad behavior, are they expecting each day to live up to the ineffable standard of "fun"? Perhaps part of what is so appealing, so fascinating about *Mad Men* is the flight from bourgeois ordinariness, the struggle against it, in all of its poetic and mundane forms.

At one point, Don Draper says to his bohemian mistress, who has no children, no husband, no obligations, "I can't decide if you have everything or nothing," and that would be the crucial question. The show seems to be managing, just barely, an existential crisis over ordinary life; it dovetails with the loopy charismatic exegesis of *The Lonely Crowd*. It asks what David Riesman called "the well heeled organization man," will you die of constraint, of boredom, of domestic propriety, or will you break out, will you run off? Don Draper, who suffers so attractively, quotes Frank O'Hara, "Now I am quietly waiting for / the catastrophe of my personality / to seem beautiful again." And one wonders if perhaps there is an audience of successful, healthy couples in the new mode, sitting in their bedrooms with flat-screen TVs waiting for just that same thing.

Today's moderately restless or mildly discontented couples tend to go to couples therapy and "work" on their relationships instead of drinking so much they don't know where they are, or slipping into a back room with a man they meet in a bar. But can we be sure our own preferred forms of malaise and alienation are better or more fruitful than theirs? Are we happier than Don and Betty Draper, or are we just doing yoga or Pilates or getting overly involved in our children's homework or "working" on our relationships?

Gay Talese, himself a scholar and connoisseur of the messy life, tells me about the early sixties at *The New York Times,* and later at *Esquire.* He remembers people keeping flasks of liquor in their desks, and recalls coming back from lunch one day and seeing one guy with his head flat down on his typewriter. No one touched him or talked to him for hours, and eventually he woke up. He also recalls copy girls slipping out in the middle of the day with more than one man to the surrounding hotels. "You didn't have the word 'exploitation' then," Mr. Talese said. "And mostly it wasn't exploitation."

And of course, the words we use create our pathologies and cast our judgments and corral us into correct or healthy behaviors: they don't allow for a huge variety of interpretation, or arguably for the full complicated range of real experience. (One such interpretation could be Oscar Wilde's: that "work is the curse of the drinking classes.") My mother recently finished a memoir about that same period in the literary circles orbiting *The Paris Review.* Reading the manuscript I was struck by how much these productive and famous writers she hung around with drank. Today we would dismiss them as alcoholics, the word itself carrying its own antiseptic morality, its own clinical, irrefutable argument for balance and sobriety, but back then it was simply charisma.

I was also struck by how many of the parties she describes, on the beach, or on the Upper East Side, devolved into romantic chaos, how easily married men fell into bed with women who were not their wives. There was a flow to an evening, a sort of dangerous possibility in the air, that would be entirely foreign at the equivalent party now, at which people generally go home with the person they are supposed to go home with. The casual and flamboyant adultery my mother describes would be judged the next morning by our healthier, more staid, more quietly unhappy couples; the cheating would be rare and furtive, and certainly not part of the ambience and festivity of, say, a book party, which is now altogether a brisker, more businesslike affair. And I don't think that in adult life most of us ever quite achieve the dissolute fluidity of those parties she describes, an atmosphere John Berryman once summarized as "Somebody slapped / Somebody's second wife somewhere."

My mother tells the story of sitting on the beach in East Hampton one morning, when my sixteen-month-old sister climbs onto the lap of a famous movie star and says, "I smell Scotch." Everybody laughs, embarrassed. My mother wonders how many sixteen-month-olds recognize the smell of Scotch on someone's breath, but by then my sister had clocked a lot of hours sleeping on the bed piled with coats at parties.

In her memoir, she also tells a story about taking my sister, who was then three, to the novelist Doc Humes's house in the middle of the night because he was having some sort of psychotic episode. She sat up with him while my sister slept on his bed, which smelled of beer and marijuana. He was seeing flames in the mirror. He was also married to someone else and had four daughters of his own. When the sun rose, my mother dropped him at Bellevue, and then continued in the cab to drop my sister off at preschool. In other words: not a style of school drop-off that most of us now would recognize.

I remember being at a *Paris Review* party at George Plimpton's house nearly four decades after my mother was one of the girls draped across the couch, when he commented dryly, "Those were wilder days when your mother was here." And the wildness he was talking about had a certain ideological cast; it was, among other things, a critique of conventional life, a refusal to accept the values of the lonely crowd, a rebellion against the well-heeled organization man. But even in literary or artistically inclined circles, our relation to mainstream bourgeois values are different now: more wishful and embracing than rebellious. Where my mother's novelist friends were determined to defy moral convention, the novelist we currently admire sells his novel to the movies, lives in a townhouse in Brooklyn, or a loft in TriBeCa, and has a good car, his bohemianism and rebellion against conventional mores basically confined to shopping at Whole Foods—with a life, in short, that suspiciously resembles that of the banker (or advertising executive) next door.

In *Mad Men* there is a scene in which Betty Draper lies in the bath reading Mary McCarthy's bestseller *The Group,* and it is McCarthy who perhaps wrote most frankly about the allure and embarrassment and comedy of the messy life. In her *Intellectual Memoirs,* which are not exactly that, she recalls one twenty-four-hour period in which she slept with three different men: "Though

slightly scared by what things were coming to, I didn't feel promiscuous. Perhaps no one ever does."

Out of curiosity I once parsed out how much McCarthy drank
in the course of a particular night: three daiquiris, two manhat-
tans, a couple of glasses of red wine, which she, by the way, refers to as "Dago Red," and then some Benedictine and brandies.
These nights often involve regret, but she writes about them with
such exuberance, such festive humor, that one can see how seductive that messiness can be.

Juxtaposed against all this flamboyance, the tameness of contemporary sins can be a little disheartening. Try telling a group
of young parents in a Draper-like milieu that you have decided to
give your baby non-organic milk instead of paying $4 for or-
ganic, or give a toddler an M&M to quiet them down in front of
a gaggle of stay-at-home moms ("they're only baby teeth," a
friend of mine once said) and see what sort of unbridled disapproval you can elicit. It seems that some of us are so busy channeling our energies into doing what is good for us, for our
children, into responsible and improving endeavors, that we may
have forgotten, somewhere in the harried trips to Express Yourself Through Theater or Trader Joe's, to seize the day. Of
course, people still have hangovers and affairs, but what dominates the wholesome vista is a sense that everything we do should
be productive, should be moving toward a sane and balanced
end, toward the dubious and fragile illusion of "healthy." The
idea that you would do something just for the momentary blissful
escape of it, for intensity, for strong feeling, is out of fashion.

When we talk about the three-martini lunch these days, it is
with a sort of dismissive contempt, tinged with a pleasurable
thrill of superiority. How much more sensible we are than them!

How much healthier! How much more prolific! "How did anyone get any work done?" someone will invariably ask. But maybe that's the wrong question, or maybe the kind of work they got done was a different kind of work, or maybe that is not the highest and holiest standard to which we can hold the quality of human life.

Of course, it's hard to write in praise of that much drinking in the middle of the day without being perverse; it's equally hard to advocate blazingly destructive affairs; it's harder still to defend the four packs of Winstons a day that Jerry Della Femina smoked in the heyday of his youth. And yet can these messy lives tell us something? Is there some adventure out there that we are not having, some vividness, some wild pleasure, that we are not experiencing in our responsible, productive days? In the seventeenth century, the metaphysical poet Andrew Marvell wrote, "But at my back I always hear / Time's winged chariot hurrying near." He also wrote, "The grave's a fine and private place, / But none, I think, do there embrace." *Mad Men* seems to be telling us the same thing, in its own stylish, made-for-television way: we are bequeathed on earth one very short life, and it might be good, one of these days, to make sure that we are living it.

The Fantasy Life of the American Working Woman

If every era gets the sadist it deserves, it may not be surprising that we have ended up with Christian Grey, the hero of *Fifty Shades of Grey*. He is not twisted or frightening or in possession of a heart of darkness; he was abused as a child, a sadist Oprah could have dreamed up. Or as E. L. James puts it, "Christian Grey has a sad side."

He is also extremely solicitous and apologetic for a sadist, always asking the book's young heroine, Anastasia Steele, about every minute gradation of her feelings, and bringing her all kinds of creams and lotions to soothe her after spanking her. He is, in other words, the easiest difficult man of all time.

Why does this particular watered-down, skinny-vanilla-latte version of sadomasochism have such cachet right now? Why did masses of women bring the book to the top of the *New York Times* bestseller list before it even hit the stores? Most likely it's the happy convergence of the superficial transgression with comfortable archetypes, the blushing virgin and the whips. To a certain, I guess rather large, population, it has a semi-pornographic glamour, a dangerous frisson of boundary crossing, but at the

same time it is delivering reassuringly safe, old-fashioned romantic roles. Reading *Fifty Shades of Grey* is no more risqué or rebellious or disturbing than, say, shopping for a pair of black boots or
an arty asymmetrical dress at Barneys.

As it happens, the prevailing stereotype of the *Fifty Shades of
Grey* reader, distilled in the condescending term "mommy porn"
as an older, suburban, possibly Midwestern woman, isn't entirely
accurate: according to the publisher's information, gleaned from
Facebook, Google searches, and fan sites, more than half the
women reading the book are in their twenties and thirties and far
more urban and blue state than the rampant caricature of them
suggests.

And of course, the current vogue for domination is not confined to surreptitious iPad reading: in Lena Dunham's acclaimed
new series, *Girls*, about twentysomethings adrift in New York
City, a similar desire for sexual submission has already emerged
as a recurring theme. The heroine's pale hipsterish ersatz boyfriend jokes, "You modern career women, I know what you like,"
and his idea, however awkwardly enacted, is that they like to be
dominated. He says things like "You should never be anyone's . . .
slave, except mine" and calls down from a window, "If you come
up I'm going to tie you up and keep you here for three days. I'm
just in that kind of mood." She comes back from seeing him with
bruises and sheepishly tells her gay college boyfriend at a bar, "I
am seeing this guy and sometimes I let him hit me on the side of
my body."

Her close friend and roommate, meanwhile, has a sweet, sensitive, respectful boyfriend in the new mold, who asks her what
she wants in bed, and she is bored out of her mind and irritated

by him; she fantasizes instead about an arrogant artist she meets at the gallery where she works, who tells her that he will scare her in bed. So nice postfeminist boys are not what these ambitious, liberal-arts-educated girls are looking for either: they are also, in their exquisitely ironic, confused way, in the market for a little creative submission.

It is intriguing that huge numbers of women are eagerly consuming disparate fantasies of submission at a moment when women are ascendant in the workplace, when they make up almost 60 percent of college students, when they are close to surpassing men as breadwinners, with four in ten working women now outearning their husbands, when the majority of women under thirty are having and supporting children on their own; a moment when, in hard economic terms, women are less dependent or subjugated than ever before.

It is probably not coincidence that, as more books like *The Richer Sex*, by Liza Mundy, and Hanna Rosin's *The End of Men* and a spate of articles on choosing not to be married or the steep rise in young women choosing single motherhood appear, there is a renewed popular interest in the stylized theater of female powerlessness. We may be especially drawn to this particular romanticized, erotically charged, semi-pornographic idea of female submission at a moment in history when male dominance is shakier than it has ever been.

In the realm of private fantasy, the allure of sexual submission, even in its extremes, is remarkably widespread. An analysis of twenty studies published in *Psychology Today* estimates that between roughly a third and 57 percent of women entertain fantasies in which they are forced to have sex. "Rape fantasies are a place where politics and Eros meet, uneasily," says Daniel Bergner, who is working on a book on female desire. "It is where what we say and what is stand next to each other, mismatched." The researchers and psychologists he talked to for a *New York Times* article, "What Do Women Want?," often seemed reluctant to even use the phrase "rape fantasy." The idea of rape fantasies was clearly making even them, the chroniclers and scholars of these fantasies, extremely nervous and apologetic. Even though fantasies are something that, by definition, one can't control, they seem to be saying something about modern women that nearly everyone wishes wasn't said. One of the researchers he interviewed preferred to call them "fantasies of submission," and another said, "It's the wish to be beyond will, beyond thought."

But why, for women especially, would free will be a burden? Why is it appealing to think of a given night in the passive tense? Why is it so interesting to surrender, or to play at surrendering? It may be that power is not always that comfortable, even for those of us who grew up in it; it may be that equality is something we want only sometimes and in some places and in some arenas; it may be that power and all of its imperatives can be boring.

In *Girls*, Lena Dunham's character finds herself for a moment lying on a gynecologist's table perversely fantasizing about having AIDS because it would free her from ambition, from responsibility, from the daunting need to make something of her life. It's a great scene, a vivid piece of real-seeming weirdness, which raises the question: Is there something exhausting about the relentless responsibility of a contemporary woman's life, about the pressure of economic participation, about all that strength and independence and desire and going out into the world? It may be that, for some, the more theatrical fantasies of sexual surrender offer a release, a vacation, an escape from the dreariness and hard work of equality.

Which is not to say that baroque stories of sexual submission are new. Sadomasochism is, of course, what someone I know referred to as "a hearty perennial." It has always existed in secret pockets, and periodically some small glimmer of it breaks into mainstream culture and fascinates us. But the S&M classics of the past make fewer compromises with normal life; they don't traffic in things as banal or ordinary as love.

In *Story of O*, the famous French novel written by Pauline Réage in 1954, the heroine is elaborately trained to be a slave, after being whisked off to a chateau where masked men whip her and abuse her sexually. O's masochism begins as an intense devotion to her lover but quickly turns into something else. O begins to vacate herself; she loses her personality in the pure discipline of pain. When Susan Sontag wrote about O, she talked about "the voluptuous yearning toward the extinction of one's consciousness."

Every so often a book or movie comes along that absorbs us and generates discussion about bondage and power, with eroticized scenes of rape or colorful submission, such as *The Ages of Lulu, Belle de Jour,* and *The Sexual Life of Catherine M.* What is interesting is that this material still, in our jaded porn-saturated age, manages to be titillating or controversial or newsworthy. We still seem to want to debate or interrogate or voyeuristically absorb scenes of extreme sexual submission. Even though we are, at this point, extremely familiar with sadomasochism, it still seems to strike the culture as new, as shocking, as overturning certain values, because something in it still feels, to a surprisingly large segment of our tolerant post-sexual-revolution world, wrong or shameful.

One of the salient facts about *Fifty Shades of Grey*'s Anastasia Steele is that she is not into sadomasochism, she is just in love with Christian Grey ("Deep down I would just like more: more affection, more playful Christian, more . . . love"), so she is willing to give beatings and leather crops the old college try. This is important for a mainstream heroine appealing to mainstream readers: she indulges in the slightly out-there fantasy of whipping and humiliation without actually taking responsibility for any off-kilter desires. She can enjoy his punishments and leather whips and mild humiliations without ever having to say that she sought them out or chose them. It's not that she wants to be whipped, it's that she willingly endures it out of love for, and maybe in an effort to save, a handsome man. This little trick of the mind, of course, is one of the central aspects of sexual submission: you can experience it without claiming responsibility, without committing to actually wanting it, which has a natural appeal to both our puritan past and our post-ironic present.

When Maggie Gyllenhaal appeared in *Secretary*, a comic commentary on a boss disciplining his secretary, she was worried about a feminist reaction against the flamboyant depiction of sexual domination. But she said, "I found women, especially of my generation, are moved by it in some way that goes beyond politics."

Explaining the endurance of submissive sexual fantasies, the feminist Katha Pollitt says, "Women have more sexual freedom

and more power than ever before in our history, but that does not
mean they have a lot of either, and it doesn't mean they don't
have complicated feelings of guilt, shame and unworthiness."
And over the years researchers and psychologists have theorized
that women harbor elaborate fantasies about sexual submission
because they feel guilty or skittish about claiming responsibility
for their own desires: they are more comfortable being wanted
than wanting, in other words. But more recent studies show that
the women who fantasize about being forced to have sex are actually less prone to guilt than those who don't. In any event, that
theory seems too sweeping or at least too nineteenth-century an
answer for most modern women: it is not so much guilt over sex
but rather something more basically liberating in the situation of
being overcome or overpowered. The thrill here is irrational, untouched by who one is in life, immune to the critical or sensible
voice, the fine education, or good job.

Feminists have long tried to explain away our continuing in-
vestment in this fantasy, the residual desire to be controlled or
dominated in the romantic sphere. They have blamed the pornographic male-dominated culture for how many strong, successful, independent women are caught up in elaborate fantasies of
submission (and realities, of course, but that's another story).
Gloria Steinem writes that these women "have been raised to believe that sex and domination are synonymous," and we must
learn to "finally untangle sex and aggression." But maybe sex and
aggression should not, and probably more to the point, cannot be
untangled.

Recently on talk shows there has been a certain amount of
upstanding feminist tsk-tsking about the retrograde soft-core ex-

ploitation of women in *Fifty Shades of Grey,* and there seems to be no shortage of liberal pundits asking, "Is this what they went to the barricades for?" But of course, the barricades have always been oddly irrelevant to intimate life.

As the brilliant feminist thinker Simone de Beauvoir answered when someone asked her if her subjugation to Jean-Paul Sartre in her personal life was at odds with her feminist theories: "Well, I just don't give a damn. . . . I'm sorry to disappoint all the feminists, but you can say it's too bad so many of them live only in theory instead of in real life."

In her controversial and revealing meditation on her own obsession with spanking in *The New Yorker,* Daphne Merkin speculates about the tension between her identity as a "formidable" woman and her yearning for a sexualized childish punishment. She writes, "Equality between men and women, or even the pretext of it, takes a lot of work and may not in any case be the surest route to sexual excitement."

It is perhaps inconvenient for feminism that the erotic imagination does not submit to politics or even changing demographic realities; it doesn't care about the End of Men or peruse feminist blogs in its spare time; it doesn't remember the hard work and dedication of the suffragettes and assorted other picket sign wavers. The incandescent fantasy of being dominated or overcome by a man shows no sign of vanishing with equal pay for equal work, and may in fact gain in intensity and take new, inventive— or, in the case of *Fifty Shades of Grey,* not so inventive—forms.

In fact, if I were a member of the Christian right, sitting on my front porch decrying the decadent morals of American working women, what would be most alarming to me about the *Fifty Shades of Grey* phenomenon, what gives it its true edge of desperation and end-of-the-world ambience, is that millions of otherwise intelligent women are willing to tolerate prose on this level. If you are willing to slog through sentences like "In spite of my poignant sadness, I laugh," or "My world is crumbling around me into a sterile pile of ashes, all my hopes and dreams cruelly dashed," you must really, really want to get to the submissive sex scene.

Is Maureen Dowd Necessary?

Maureen Dowd's penchant for provocative overstatement found its natural outlet in her book *Are Men Necessary?* In it she bemoans a perceived return of 1950s values and courtship rituals and portrays a younger generation of women as grasping, shallow housewife wannabes. In the most inflammatory and intriguing passages, she claims that men are put off by women in power, that they prefer the women who serve them, "maids, masseuses, and secretaries," to their equals. She goes on to attribute the fact that she herself is unmarried to her powerful position as an op-ed columnist at *The New York Times*. At one point, she notes her own family history of domestic service and concludes that being a maid would have enhanced her chances with men.

Is this dark view of sexual politics a little extreme? If it is, it shouldn't be surprising. Dowd pushes every statement to its most exaggerated form; her column occupies a space somewhere in between the other columns on the *New York Times* op-ed page and the political cartoons that sometimes run there. She is, at her best, a brilliant caricaturist of the political scene, turning each presidency into vivid farce. As a caricaturist, she has a fondness for punchy one-liners strung together, and for the one-sentence paragraph: "Survival of the fittest has been replaced by survival of the fakest"; "We had the Belle Epoque. Now we have the Botox Epoch"; and "As a species is it possible that men are ever so last century?" Her style evokes a brainier Candace Bushnell, whose oeuvre she frequently refers to, but it is given extra weight by her position at the *Times*.

Like the crude, sexist men she obsessively lampoons, Dowd is extremely fond of clever stereotyping. But this strategy is better suited to satirizing a real person (say, President Bush) than it is to offering insights into the already cartoonish war between the sexes. In *Are Men Necessary?* she gravitates toward quotes like this: "Deep down all men want the same thing: a virgin in a gingham dress," or "if there's one thing men fear it's a woman who uses her critical faculties." To support these generalizations, Dowd relies on the faux journalism of women's magazines. She cobbles together anecdotal evidence from people she encounters. The formula is basically this: "Carrie, a twenty-nine-year-old publicist, says . . ." And from Carrie's experience she extrapolates to the universal. The problem with this approach, of course, is that one could go out and find a twenty-nine-year-old publicist who would say the opposite. It would be one thing if Dowd were writing pure, straightforward polemic, ranting against the people she feels the need to rant against, but Dowd is pretending to cover cultural trends with journalistic accuracy, and it is this pretense that gives her arguments a shoddy, makeshift feel.

Much of what Dowd observes in the piece is true: the nostalgic passion for the 1950s, the increasing number of educated women opting to be housewives or change their names when they marry, the strange, runaway success of books like *The Rules*.

And yet, somehow, the alarmist portrait she draws of female life feels skewed. Her sensationalism renders the generation she is writing about unrecognizable. She seems to believe that we are all obsessed with beauty, we all want to efface our personalities to ensnare a man, we all want to stay home and take care of him.

In fact, Dowd's most compelling example of the rarefied, lonely demographic of woman too successful for love is herself.

As Dowd would have it, men simply find her intelligence, her status, her wit too daunting. (A friend called her up to complain that her own Pulitzer Prize would make it impossible for her to get a date.) But is it possible that there is something else at play? In a recent *New York* profile, the writer reports: "She is an utter and unreconstructed fox. Something that nearly every person I spoke to about her mentioned, unprompted, is that men can't resist her." The piece further describes the wide variety of men Dowd has been involved with, ranging from movie stars, to important editors, to creators of television dramas. And they have apparently all been attracted to her, even though she is not in a service profession, or a maid, or a virgin in a gingham dress. One imagines that her intelligence, her sharpness, her sarcasm, may even have interested or enticed these men. Could there possibly be another reason that the attractive, successful Dowd has not settled down? Something that is not in the zeitgeist, or the political climate, but some irreducible quality of her own psychology? It would seem wrong to raise this question about a woman writer, and in fact about any writer, but Dowd uses her experience with men as a template for her theories so often, and marshals her failure to marry as evidence so frequently, that she herself plants the question in her reader's mind.

One of Dowd's many admirers extravagantly compared her

to Edith Wharton. But Wharton was among the first female writers to write about the single woman's ambivalence toward marriage, a subject Dowd conspicuously evades. What is maddening about Dowd's book and the excerpt in *The New York Times Magazine* is that she does not develop her ideas, that she does not push beneath the surface. One wishes that, instead of devoting herself to zinginess, to ripostes and one-liners, she would use her threatening intelligence to unearth the deeper complexities of her subject. Is there something about the generation of women who came of age in the late 1960s "in male-dominated universities and workplaces" that finds its own power unsettling? Why is it that so many women are taking refuge in outdated visions of femininity?

I don't mean to suggest that there is something inherently wrong with using one's own life in political writing. But one should use it honestly, rigorously, complicatedly, like critics such as Mary McCarthy, Rebecca West, Joan Didion, Christopher Hitchens, or Andrew Sullivan. Because the issues surrounding sexual politics are so emotionally charged, so laden with contradiction, so racked with ambivalence and irrationality, it is especially important not to neglect nuance. One of the failures of the feminist movement in the first place was a reliance on easy aphorisms, and the schematic worldview that such aphorisms implied or evoked. The famous line "A woman without a man is like a fish without a bicycle" did not prove to be a constructive or interesting contribution to the feminist cause. Replacing one set of rigid gender stereotypes with another did not allow women the full range of their desires and ended up sabotaging and satirizing the movement. Dowd herself criticizes the feminists of the 1970s for imagining a sea of identical, sexless women in navy blazers descending on the workplace. Though she appears to be arguing for a new, more rigorous feminism, she is guilty of precisely the same intellectual fault, starting with the catchy meaningless title of her book, *Are Men Necessary?* Dowd's aphorisms, amusing and pithy in the morning paper along with a cup of coffee, are precisely what the conversation about sexual politics does not need.

Profiles Encouraged

In the spring of 2000, a freelance writer named Tom Kummer was caught fabricating movie star profiles for one of Germany's most respected newspapers, *Süddeutsche Zeitung.* He wrote graceful articles about stars he had never met. He had been doing it for years. *The Times* of London reported that his interviews were so good that *Marie Claire* interviewed him about "the secrets of his success," which he ironically said was demanding at least forty-five minutes with his subjects. What eventually betrayed him was his inability to be banal, his desire to put ideas into people's mouths that they would never actually utter. In other words, his fatal mistake was to make the celebrity profile interesting. *The Times* of London reported that he had Sharon Stone saying she is trying "to irritate men from wholly different classes of society," and Courtney Love saying she felt "empty, depressed, rather dumb." The fact that he was able to carry on for so long tells us less about Kummer than it does about the genre itself. The style of celebrity profiles has become so rigid, so absolutely predictable, that the substance, the poor ephemeral star herself, is wholly superfluous. That was the piece of information

Tom Kummer passed along, the valuable contribution he made to the journalistic community, the point he dramatized as no one had before: *All movie star profiles are the same.*

Our celebrity culture has become so greedy and wild that it overwhelms and consumes the writer's individual voice. It feels, sometimes, like the writer gives up, thinks of the rent bill, and types on a kind of automatic pilot, giving the magazine or the reader or the movie publicists what they want—and nothing more. Our appetite for the same photograph of a movie star in a spaghetti-strap dress is insatiable, and so, it seems, is our appetite for the same article.* But why are we interested in these articles when we could generate them from thin air as easily as Tom Kummer? It may be because the celebrity profile is not about information, it is not about journalism, it is not about words; it is a ritual.

No matter who the celebrity is, the pieces follow the same narrative arc. There is the moment when the movie star reveals himself to be just like us. (In *Vanity Fair*, "Pitt, then, turns out to be that most surprising of celebrities—a modest man" and "Paltrow jumps up to clear the table and has to be told almost sternly not to do the dishes.") There is the moment when the movie star is not

---

*I wrote this piece before the blossoming of celebrity websites, but the endurance of the genre is even more impressive than when I wrote about it here. Even if we can now easily and instantaneously obtain a tiny little nugget of love and hate from gossip sites, the culture maintains its mysterious appetite for the long-form magazine profile, with all of its trite conventions. These profiles have not changed substantively since the advent of the Internet, and if you open a *Vanity Fair* or *In Style* in the dentist's office, you will witness the same clichés at work. The fact that the Internet has not had more effect on the movie star profile betrays a lot about the nature of the ritual: it is not news or information that is the profile's true purpose. Our reasons for reading them, then and now, are largely ritualistic and wholly independent from what could be called content.

mortal after all. (In *Entertainment Weekly*, Julia Roberts has "a long, unbound mass of chocolate-brown curls—just the kind of Julia Roberts waterfall tangle of tresses that makes America think of bumper crops and Wall Street rallies and $100 million at the box office.") There is the fact that the movie star was funny-looking and gawky as a child ("I had braces, and I was skinny," says Gwyneth Paltrow in *People*.) There is the J. D. Salinger book the movie star is reading (*Entertainment Weekly* reports that Julia Roberts "has a book of J. D. Salinger stories . . . on the coffee table," and Winona Ryder tells *In Style*, "I have every edition, every paperback, every translation of *The Catcher in the Rye*"). And then there is the moment when the author of the piece wryly acknowledges the artificiality of the situation. ("I have firm instructions from your people to make you comfortable," a *Harper's Bazaar* writer says to Brad Pitt, "so perhaps you should choose where you'd like to sit.") There is the disbelief on the part of both the celebrity and the author about how rich and famous and successful the movie star has become. In the end, it's not hard to see why Tom Cruise might not be all that essential to a Tom Cruise profile. With the pieces themselves as strictly styled as a geisha's makeup, the face behind them ceases to matter.

Start with the way the movie star looks. How should the aspiring plagiarist describe her? What should she be wearing? In *Esquire*, Winona Ryder was "in jeans, cowboy boots, and a clingy Agnes B.–type jersey," in *Life* she was "in jeans and a long-sleeved undershirt," and in *In Style* she was "makeup-free, hair swept up in a headband." In *Harper's Bazaar*, Gwyneth Paltrow "is wearing jeans, a blue cotton-fleece sweatshirt. . . . Her hair is held back by a wide black headband," and in *Vanity Fair*, she wears "her long blond hair pulled back in a simple ponytail and no trace of makeup." Julia Roberts wears "Levi's, a snug blue top. . . . Her hair is pulled back" in *Vanity Fair* and "Levi's, a white shirt, boots, and no makeup" in *In Style*. In *Vanity Fair*, Renée Zellweger wears "jeans, a T-shirt, sneakers, and no makeup." A stripped-down wardrobe is offered as proof of the stars' unpretentiousness, their surprising accessibility.

If glossy magazines are to be believed, movie stars also have a limited number of character traits, one of which is vulnerability. Somebody in nearly every profile comments on that surprising aspect of the fabulous person's psyche, and if somebody else doesn't, the writer will. The mother of Jack Nicholson's child, for instance, is quoted in *Cosmopolitan* as saying that Nicholson is "very strong yet very vulnerable." Julia Roberts is described in *Vanity Fair* as being "boldly vulnerable," and in *Cosmopolitan*, "her vulnerability brought Marilyn Monroe to mind," whereas in *Good Housekeeping*, "that same vulnerability that made her a star almost destroyed her." In *Rolling Stone*, she "show[s] some vulnerability." In *Vanity Fair*, Meg Ryan has a "compelling vulnerability," and Rupert Everett says of Madonna, "She has a lot of vulnerability"; in *The New Yorker*, Regis Philbin is described by a fan as "totally vulnerable." And why not? Vulnerability is the natural counterpoint to the sublime perfection that the profiler has gone out of his way to chronicle. It is a vague way of satisfying the need for the movie star to be "human" without detracting from her glamour with undue or distracting specificity.

And then there is the physical illustration of vulnerability: the mere presence of a magazine writer makes actresses turn every shade of red. In *Vanity Fair*, Renée Zellweger is "pink," and Meg Ryan's "face flushes." In *Harper's Bazaar*, Gwyneth Paltrow's "cheeks flush"; in a *Vanity Fair* article, she "concedes with a blush"; and in a *Vogue* article, "Paltrow turns crimson." *Esquire* reports a story in which Winona Ryder "turns scarlet." In *Newsweek*, the mention of her boyfriend's name causes Julia Roberts to blush, and in *In Style*, it "reduced her to almost girlish blushes." Even Madonna blushes in *Vanity Fair.*

Not only do they blush; they glow. *Redbook* gushes, "It's really true: when you see Julia Roberts in person, she just . . . glows." *Vanity Fair* refers to her as "a lovely young woman glowing amid the flashbulbs," and *People* says, "Fans can't get enough of her glowing face." In *Newsweek*, the writer doesn't think Gwyneth Paltrow needs to lighten her hair because "she's glowing already," and *Vogue* rhapsodizes about her "big, glowing smile." Other hackneyed phrases pop up regularly: in *Good Housekeeping*, Julia Roberts is "like the proverbial deer caught in headlights," and in *Vanity Fair*, Meg Ryan "looked like a deer in headlights." There is no need in movie star profiles to dispense with clichés because clichés—red carpet, flashbulbs, incandescence—are what stardom consists of: the role of the movie star profile is to reinforce and sell that stardom, not to examine or undermine it. Which is also why almost all movie star profiles from *People* to *The New Yorker* are peppered with superlatives—they add to the breathiness of the piece, the tone of worshipful trashy love and sheer commerce. *Cosmopolitan* calls Julia Roberts "the most desirable and successful actress in the world." *Redbook* calls her "the biggest female star on the planet." And *People* declares that "Roberts is, quite simply, the most appealing actress of her time." In *Vogue*, Gwyneth Paltrow is "The Luckiest Girl Alive," and in *Time* she is "the most beguiling actress of her young generation." In *The New Yorker*, Tom Hanks is "the most disarming and successful of American movie stars." In *People*, Brad Pitt is

"Hollywood's hottest hunk," and Tom Cruise is "The Sexiest Man Alive." It is rare that one reads about a moderately success-ful actress, or the second-sexiest man in Hollywood.

Every actress over the age of twenty is also depicted as girlish, childlike, or adolescent. Take the description of Julia Roberts in *Vanity Fair* ("by turns childlike and sophisticated"), or Renée Zellweger (who has "little-girl moxie") in *Vanity Fair*, or Meg Ryan ("whose adult allure is redolent of adolescence") in *Vanity Fair*, or Sharon Stone (whose "childlike sexual greediness was perhaps the most eerily enticing quality about her *[Basic] Instinct* work"), also in *Vanity Fair*. In *In Style*, the then twenty-eight-year-old Winona Ryder is like a "defiant teen," and in *Life* she "sits like a kid." Fifty-something Goldie Hawn, *In Style* informs us, looks as "youthful as a teenager," and a look of "childlike glee overtakes" Julia Roberts. *Cosmopolitan* compares Madonna to a "restless child," while *Vanity Fair* describes "the little girl . . . be-hind the woman." Male actors are invariably described as boyish. "Part of Hanks's appeal," *The New Yorker* explained, "is his boy-ishness." *GQ* talks about how Tom Cruise "projects a sexuality that is boyish." Even Warren Beatty appears "tousled and boy-ish" in *The New York Times Magazine*.

It often seems that the writers of magazine profiles have spent one too many Saturday nights watching *Breakfast at Tiffany's* on late-night cable, because nearly every movie star is compared to Audrey Hepburn or Holly Golightly, as Charlize Theron is in *Vanity Fair* and Julia Ormond is in *The New York Times Maga-zine*. In *Newsweek*, Gwyneth Paltrow's neck "brings Audrey Hepburn to mind," and other qualities of hers provoke the same comparison in *Vogue* and *In Style*. Julia Roberts is compared to Audrey Hepburn in both *In Style* and in *Vanity Fair* twice, and

Redbook reports that "she is the only actress now who can lay claim to Audrey Hepburn's mantle."

It is increasingly common for a magazine profile to include a pious denunciation or mockery of the tabloids, where, the highbrow writer points out, every little thing the celebrity does is being followed, every detail of what she eats and whom she dates is being observed—what an outrage to human dignity and privacy! And yet one wonders how the *Vanity Fair* or *Vogue* or *Entertainment Weekly* article is so wildly different. Indeed, it is often the same gossip, the same mundane details wrapped up and delivered in a different tone. But highbrow writers, and even not-so-highbrow writers, continue to be outraged by the tabloids, as if a slightly more literary turn of phrase changes the fundamental moral tenor and cultural worthiness of the venture. The anti-tabloid or anti-paparazzi moment serves a definite function: it justifies the profile as more than just gossip. One writer in *Vanity Fair* makes fun of an item from the *New York Post* about Julia Roberts eating brunch with Benjamin Bratt at Caffe Lure on Sullivan Street, and then proceeds to report in all seriousness that she shops for soy milk at Korean delis. The qualitative difference between these two observations is unclear. It may be a certain amount of self-contempt projected onto the "tabloids" for their invasive curiosity, or it may be that the highbrow writer really believes that his pursuit is more legitimate simply because it is juxtaposed with such psychological insights as "she's no shrinking violet" and printed on higher-quality paper.

There are certain stylistic guidelines that immediately present themselves to the aspiring plagiarist. One of the transparent rhetorical tricks employed by movie star profilers across the country is a hip, *Bright Lights, Big City,* second-person voice. A *Newsweek* profile of Julia Roberts states, "On the way to her house, Roberts drags you into a lingerie shop and tries to persuade you to buy a nightgown for your wife." And in *Entertainment Weekly,* "As you walk in the door, Roberts tells you she's in her panic state." In *Rolling Stone,* "what really throws you is what happens when Cruise puts the pedal to the metal." This is a cheap way of drawing the reader into the encounter: offering the illusion that it is you who is admiring the view with the luminous cluster of glamour that is Brad Pitt. So much of the movie star profile is premised on the perception of the reader's desperate desire to "meet" the movie star that it is no surprise that the fantasy should be so literally enacted in the style. The writer does not feel called upon to make the scene so vivid that we feel as if we are there; instead, he lazily types out three words: *you are there.*

One of the most important moments in the movie star profile is the moment of intimacy. That is, the moment when the writer proves that he has really contacted his celestial subject and has forged a genuine connection, distinguishing himself from the sycophantish hordes and servers-up of celebrity fluff. In *The New York Times Magazine,* the profiler writes, "Minutes after the plane lands, Ormond and I are slumped in the backseat of a limousine. We're tired. We're angry. We are about to have our first fight." Or it can be something smaller, along the lines of this Julia Roberts profile in *Newsweek:* "Later she takes your arm. And crosses Union Square." Or this one in *Vogue:* "One last hug. Paltrow, after two hours of fashion madness, smells very eau de fresh." Or it can be a flirtatious voice-mail message, like the one Regis Philbin leaves a *New Yorker* writer: "(The next day I received a message on my voice mail: 'Spend a whole day with you. Sing my guts out onstage for you. And not even a goodbye.')" The writer reports the flirtation, the few seconds of intimacy, the subtext of which is that he or she has really made an impression on the star, has penetrated the defenses. In *The New York Times Magazine,* the writer says that Warren Beatty "studied the artifacts of my life as if they were long-lost Mayan ruins." Julia Roberts says to a *Vanity Fair* writer, "You've got a pretty good pair of lips there yourself." These flirtations are never offered as evidence of the star's manipulative powers or professional charm, but rather suggest the ability of this particularly appealing and attractive writer to get beyond the routine and glitter and impress the real person.

In a *Vanity Fair* profile of Renée Zellweger, "the look on her face is one that a grown woman gets that lets a man know that the night is now over." Often, the sexual overtone, the very datiness of the interview, is played up by the writer. It is fawning fandom taken to its logical extreme. There is a flirtation between the interviewer and the interviewee, a play of power, an adoration mingled with hostility that resembles nothing more than a high school courtship. Here is *Vanity Fair*'s Kevin Sessums, the consummate highbrow profile writer and provocateur, with Julia Roberts: " 'You're famous because you're a good actress. You're infamous because of the actors you've f—ked,' I challenged, trying to shock a response from her. Roberts flashed her eyes at me the way she can flash them on-screen when someone has gotten her attention. Seduction lay in her un-shockable stare; she cocked her head and waited." One can hear what he is saying to the reader: I have gotten Julia Roberts's attention! Seduction lay in her stare! But comments like this are often laced with a sadism— a certain resentment, perhaps, of having to sit there with an important person and record every minor dietary habit you are lucky enough to observe—that makes its way into the prose.

Take the moment Sessums says to Meg Ryan, " 'Cocaine may harden one's heart, but it makes one, well, less hard in other places,' I venture. 'If you were intimate with him—and I assume you were—how could you not know he was snorting coke?' "

Because fawning laced with irony somehow seems cooler and more palatable, the paradox of writers like Kevin Sessums—who has written more than thirty celebrity profiles for *Vanity Fair* alone—emerges. The tone is knowing and flirtatious and world-weary. But what is strange is how the world-weariness meshes with naïve fascination. It is, in a way, a perfect reflection of the culture—a faux-intellectual distance masquerading as the real thing. Irony that is really adoration in a new form. The complexities of the tone make celebrity worship less demeaning, giving it a kind of chic allure it would not otherwise have. These complexities allow the intelligent, critical reader to interest herself in the exact beige of the movie star's furniture, to read about the blush and glow without shame. There is often a stunned incredulity, tinged with sexual attraction, that seems to render the writer comparatively speechless, so that the profile is dotted with banal statements of wonder that seem out of place in otherwise competent writing, as when a *Vanity Fair* reporter quotes Madonna as saying, "I wanted to be somebody," and then adds, "And boy is she." That "boy is she" would not have made it into a piece about Hillary Clinton or Michael Bloomberg; its wide-eyed wonderment would not have a place in any form of journalism other than that of the celebrity profile. It's as if the presence of Madonna had dazzled and almost drugged the writer (and the reader) into a haze of inarticulateness, a baby patter of awe.

But why are we willing to put up with it, to wade through the stock phrases, to pick up the same articles on the newsstand again and again? Especially now when the Internet offers up any "news" the long-form profile might have once yielded? When we can consume in a few seconds the photographs or gossip on an iPhone on the subway? Why do we still read a profile in *Vanity Fair*? Because, in the end, we are not interested in Angelina Jolie; we are interested in fame: its pure, bright, disembodied effervescence. And what these articles do is strip down the particulars to give us the excitement itself. They provide us with the affect of excitement, the sound and feel of it. It is a primitive thing, this form of admiration, one that paints in fuzzy lines and speaks in hackneyed terms. True mystery doesn't interest us; the statement "she had an aura of mystery" does. The clichés are what we crave and continue to expect. What makes glamour like lights on a marquee is the repetition of the familiar sounds of adoration, the same babble of fawning irony, the same vulnerable perfect creature we don't really want to read about.

Elect Sister Frigidaire

At some point in the course of her colorful and doomed presidential campaign, I notice that I haven't met or encountered a single woman who likes Hillary Clinton.* They may agree with her politics, may think that she would be an effective leader, may support her candidacy for president, but they don't like her. Most express this unfortunate state of affairs with a resigned and mildly regretful air. "Like," of course, is a slippery and complicated word; it shields us from the responsibilities and revelations of our preferences. It allows us to hide from our own feelings: it is as mysterious and ineffable and outside of ourselves as physical attraction or love. What can we do? Would that it were otherwise! But we just don't *like* her. We like her husband, but we don't like her.

---

* Now that Hillary Clinton has receded into a semi-visible hardworking political role, she is less of a lightning rod than she once was. People can admire her, in a cool or distant way. The controversy of her personality has died down into a sort of dull, and possibly begrudging, respect and is certainly tied more specifically to her political actions. There seems to be something about the platform of presidential politics, with its high stakes and shimmering symbolism, that brought out the dislike and suspicion and competitiveness I chronicle here.

We don't know her, of course, though we know people like her. To be fair, our impression of her comes from a conglomeration of newspaper clippings and television appearances and photographs in our heads, a hologram, a fantasy, a mystical conjunction, a quirky coalescence of a million tiny experiences of our own with the news. When Bill Clinton was running for president in the early 1990s, I was in school, and everywhere there were fashionable badges and buttons: HILLARY FOR PRESIDENT. In those days, the outlandish, sly slogan had a certain allure: the improbable, humorous point, the flashy rhetorical gesture. And yet as soon as there is a distinct possibility that Hillary could in fact *be* president, there is a marked lack of enthusiasm surrounding the prospect.

Years ago the *New York Post* ran a column entitled "Just What Is It About a Phony like Hillary Clinton That Makes My Skin Crawl?" And the word "phony" is the key to a certain strain of animosity against Hillary. It is no longer a revelation that politicians are phonies, that the perfection and refinement and deployment of phoniness is in fact politics at its best. Vast swaths of the country are entirely conversant in the language of spin, completely at home with the constant attempt to describe the mechanism of phoniness, the creation of political character that is everywhere in the news. In fact, integral to the entertainment of the political scene is watching the aides and consultants spin, and the discussion and analysis of that spin. And so: Why should it matter, why should it make our skin crawl, that Hillary Clinton in particular is a phony? Or rather, what is it about her specific brand of phoniness that irks us?

The distrust that many express toward Hillary nearly always returns to the vexed and unresolvable question of her relation to

Bill Clinton. The central manifestation of her phoniness appears to be her marriage, which many persist in viewing as an "arrangement," a word which began cropping up as early as the Gennifer Flowers scandal. The implication is that Hillary is so interested, so pathologically invested in politics that somewhere along the line she made a "deal" that she would tolerate her husband's infidelities. A Republican strategist once referred to the Clintons' marriage as a "merger" and this sense of the deal, of the business transaction, of the chilly conglomeration of powers, lingers in the public imagination. When Hillary offended a country singer and her fans by saying on *60 Minutes,* after the Gennifer Flowers incident, "I'm not sitting here, some little woman standing by my man like Tammy Wynette," she in fact offended a much broader group by the implication that she was not tolerating her husband's affairs just because she felt the same sort of pathetic, self-effacing love other more ordinary women feel; she was tolerating them because of their *shared political goals.*

In fact, for a brief time, it seemed that her husband's womanizing could be a perverse gift to Hillary's public image. As the Lewinsky scandal broke, Hillary enjoyed a brief but definite surge in popularity. She appeared on the cover of *Vogue.* She was dignified, yet hurt, a stance we seem to enjoy in our first ladies. But when she started talking about the "vast right-wing conspiracy" one morning on the *Today* show, she dipped in likeability again. She was back on message. The personal was political. This seemed a jarring and unforgivable swerve away from the story that was supposed to be about intimate and recognizable things like betrayal and pain. Was politics all this woman could think about?

In the wake of the Lewinsky scandal, there was much speculation about whether Hillary was somehow complicit in her husband's affairs. The summer after the impeachment hearings
brought emergent rumors that Hillary faked being mad at the
president, that she wouldn't hold his hand on her way to a vacation on Martha's Vineyard as part of a deliberately staged effort
to appear angry. She was pretending to be hurt because she knew
it would play well with the American public, that it would hu-
manize her. While this scenario seems wildly improbable, the
fantasy itself is revealing: the idea that she may not have suffered
from Clinton's infidelities was much more disturbing than the
idea that she had. A widely circulated anecdote from the sensational book *State of a Union: Inside the Complex Marriage of Bill
and Hillary Clinton*, by Jerry Oppenheimer, fed into similar sus-
picions. It described a letter she allegedly wrote to Clinton before
they were married: "I know all of your little girls are around
there. If that is what this is, you will outgrow this. Remember
what we've talked about. Remember the goals we've set for ourselves. You keep trying to stray from the plan we've put together." The lingering sense that she might have signed on for
the life that she was in fact living was, for some reason, unforgivable. Did she know that he was going to cheat on her? Did she
choose to marry him anyway? The possibility that she was in a
marriage whose narrative was not centrally about love, or at least
monogamous love, informed the image of her as cold, inhuman,
a virago, a *phony*.

Indeed, the question looms over every book about Hillary:
How motivated by power and ambition is she? Precisely how de-
tached is she from what we consider the normal human emo-

tions? Hillary herself comments wryly on this when, in *Living History*, she writes, "Some people were eager to see me in the flesh and decide for themselves whether or not I was a normal human being." A certain hardness, an independence, an ambition in all her endeavors, has always struck observers. Her high school yearbook predicted that Hillary Rodham would become a nun called "Sister Frigidaire." And this idea of her as mannish, cold, clung to her. One of the Hillary books, *Her Way: The Hopes and Ambitions of Hillary Rodham Clinton*, by Jeff Gerth and Don Van Natta, Jr., includes a dark, paranoid account of the "plan" in which each of the Clintons occupies the White House for eight years. And the image of the "deal" continued to shadow the discussion long after Bill Clinton left the White House. When Hillary ran for the U.S. Senate, it seemed to many as if this too might be part of the "deal." This prospect is often cited as part of her fakery, her sham marriage, even though this sort of deal, on more minor levels, and in more subtle ways, takes place in marriage all the time.

As a thought experiment, let us say that Hillary was in fact all the things that she is accused of being, that all of the most sinister accusations against her involving "plans" and "pacts" were true. Let us say that the idea is that she is using her marriage as a vehicle for power, that she was from the beginning attracted to Bill Clinton because she knew he would bring her closer to the center of power. Let's say she was one of those people for whom love, erotic attachment, and all of its attendant pain was secondary to her desire to run the world. Let us say that all of what she herself calls "the brittle caricatures" of her are true. Why should unnatural ambition be so alarming in a presidential candidate? Why should the single-minded pursuit of power at the cost of all per-

sonal relations be so unlikeable? Why shouldn't we want Sister
Frigidaire for president?

Hillary's drive, her ambition, her hard work, her deft manipulation of power, her refusal to be vulnerable, her unwillingness to
allow love to get in the way of career goals, at least in her mature
years, could be seen, if anything, as a sign of strength. She is in
many ways the feminist dream incarnate, the opportunity made
flesh. Surely if one had said to a group of women waving picket
signs in the 1970s, "One day there will be a presidential candidate
as ruthless, as cold, as willing to sacrifice relationships for power
as any man," they would have been heartened. And yet, even our
admiration for her undeniable achievements has a chilly aspect,
an abstract, pro forma quality. If Clinton is in many ways the
embodiment of certain feminist ideals, then it may be that many
of us don't like feminism in its purest form.

It is interesting to note that in spite of predictions to the con-
trary, Hillary has a much more comfortable relation to younger,
blue-collar women, a much more effortless popularity. It is, paradoxically, the women most like her, the demographic most similar in their education and achievements, that have the most
difficulty with her. This is curious. It makes one wonder whether
there is an element of competitiveness to the dislike, a question
beneath the surface: why her and not me? Strong, accomplished
women who one would think would respect her, would identify
with her, may in fact resent her. Could it be that we like the idea
of strong women, but we don't actually like strong women? If
we are being entirely honest, we have to admit that there is often
an intolerance on the part of powerful women toward other powerful women, a cattiness, a nastiness, that is not a part of any
feminist conversation I have ever heard. It is so much easier, so

much cooler, so much more appealing, to have a Hillary for President button when Hillary is not, in fact, running for president.

There is also the matter of Hillary's forced relation to femininity. Her transformation from a woman who cut her own hair and wore work shirts and jeans and no makeup to a coiffed blonde in pink cashmere and pearls has been much noted and commented on. Hillary writes in *Living History* about the arrival of stylists in her life during Clinton's first campaign: "I was like a kid in a candy store, trying out every style I could. Long hair, short hair, bangs, flips, braids and buns. This was a new universe and it turned out to be fun." But of course, one doesn't get a sense of fun from that particular passage. Here again is the phoniness. Her pleasure and mastery of traditional femininity is not effortless; rather, one feels the labor, the artifice. At one point, *Time* magazine accused her of "allowing handlers to substitute the heart of Martha Stewart for her own." And it seemed that way because her relation to all things female felt unnatural, contrived. What is interesting is that this groping for a kind of workable femininity, a palatable, mainstream feminine image, necessary as it so obviously was, bothered us. Hillary was unable to project the effortless image of a strong, yet feminine woman that the next generation, at least, has come to expect. It is meant to be easy, to be seamless, the transition from tough, serious workaholic to lady in kitten heels. It is meant to look natural, and the sheer awkwardness, the effort that Clinton projected, the contradictions that she so conspicuously, so crudely, embodied were perhaps a little close to home. She is trying too hard, and the spectacle of all this trying is uncomfortable, embarrassing. One could feel in a palpable way the smart woman's impersonation of the pretty woman, the career woman's impersonation of the stay-at-home mom; one could feel a lack of grace. This is perhaps the quandary of our particular iteration of feminism, how hard even a younger generation is trying, how often it feels faked. Hillary's "phoniness" may be so irritating, so unforgivable, to so many smart, driven, women in part because it is our own.

"Love Child"

The other afternoon, as people were gossiping about the breakup of Arnold Schwarzenegger's marriage, I found myself thinking about the origins of the ubiquitous but complicated term "love child." If the phrase was once slangy or tabloidish, news organizations ranging from *CBS News* to *The Washington Post* now seem to consider it a straightforward descriptive phrase, as if it were the Standard English term for a child born outside of marriage, which makes it seem like as fruitful a time as any to untangle its vexed etymology.

The word itself dates back to at least 1805. In *The Nuns of the Desert*, Eugenia de Acton writes of a "Miss Blenheim" being "what in that country is denominated a love-child," and the term appears again a little later in Percy Bysshe Shelley's *Posthumous Poems*. Another important addendum in the word's history is, of course, the 1968 Diana Ross and the Supremes' song "Love Child," with the truly transcendent rhyme "Love child never meant to be / Love child scorned by society."

Of course, we will never know exactly what went on between Schwarzenegger and his housekeeper, but I am quite sure that most of the pundits and commentators and gossips who are using the phrase "love child" do not think that it was "love." The ironies or elaborate commentaries within the phrase are fraught; the word "love" in this instance is in fact communicating the idea of sex, of unmade beds, of hotel rooms in the afternoon. Most people are not actually thinking, when they utter the phrase, "Oh, how nice. A love child!"

When people say that they feel sorry for Schwarzenegger's "children," or when he himself asks the media to "respect my wife and children through this extremely difficult time," I am fairly sure that they mean his legitimate children, and that no one is being asked to respect his love child, who is with that pretty little prefix "love" somehow airlifted out of both his father's familial obligations and the general moral concern.

Perhaps the *Washington Post* editor who chose to use the word "love child" as a purely descriptive phrase may have thought there was no better term, and he may be right. This may be one of those shadowy instances in which language fails us. Is there another word that does not carry with it some smirking holier-than-thou-ness, some puritanical judgment, some gleeful shades of schadenfreude? "A child born out of wedlock" is clunky, and the word "wedlock" is not exactly au courant.

The cool and technical "illegitimate" is not very nice; although at first glance it appears to be a neutral term, a *Merriam-Webster* detour around the whole messy hullabaloo, it too is freighted with an elaborate moral critique. What, one wonders, is more legitimate in the twenty-first century about the children of married people than those of people too busy, distracted, or original to be married?

Since our bigotries are less openly and exuberantly expressed than they were in past decades, they take refuge in subtle, shifting word choices. "Love child" is definitely more friendly or tactful than the more Shakespearean "bastard" or Hawthorne's "sin-born infant," but it nonetheless conveys a certain discomfort with the facts. "Love child" is both tolerant (that is, more tolerant than other terms) and mocking; it contains within it our contradictions; it passes judgment in an ironic way—indirectly, playfully, but also plainly.

Note the pictures posted in various venues of the boy in question: standing next to his mother, who is smiling in a white parka, is the boy, his head pixilated so that we can't see his face. Like all efforts to protect the privacy of those considered victims, this has the dubious effect of reinforcing the sense of shame: it puts forward the message that there is something to be ashamed of. We have to pixilate his face because we don't want people on the street to recognize him. (Here one thinks of the dictionary definition of "bastard": "Something that is of irregular, inferior or dubious origin.")

There is in all this a sense that this love child should be protected because he is, as Diana Ross says, "scorned by society."

As you read about the scandal on the Internet, it is not long before you come upon headlines like "Arnold's Secret Lovechild to Blame in Split with Maria," as if the kid himself is responsible for the collapse of the large Brentwood household. And you can't help but notice that the faces of Schwarzenegger's other four children are not blurred—because, the subliminal message goes, they would have nothing to be ashamed of if they were spotted on the street, or on an airplane, or in a Starbucks. They are simply children, not love children.

I happen to have a child outside of marriage, whom I sometimes refer to, in a half-serious, half-jesting way, as a love child, especially around other people who have children outside of marriage. Is this because this is the best term we have? Or is there a sense that we are not apologizing for our children by resorting to the silliest, most tabloidy phrase in circulation? I have a feeling that it's a little bit of both.

Stepping back, though, what is a tiny bit subversive and possibly appealing about the term is the faint suggestion that the love child has something more to do with love than the baby born in wedlock, who is in a certain sense just doing his job, fulfilling the natural and upstanding function of holy matrimony. On some level, the existence of the love child is testimony to some special energy on the planet, to someone doing something not necessarily sanctioned by the Bible, on his or her own time, out of some extra industry or aspiration.

Some might argue I am being a little overly scrupulous here. Does it matter what words we use for the child of an afternoon fling? As George Orwell wrote, "If thought corrupts language, language can also corrupt thought." Which is to say, the words we use actually shape the way we think, and not just the other way around. In these casual phrases and headlines we are spreading our attitudes, as ambivalent, confused, and inconsistent as they are; we are propagating our mixed messages, our prurient judgments, our puritan fantasies. We are, in our inimitable, ironic register, proving to the love child just how unloved he actually is.

Considering the growing number of children born outside the institution of holy matrimony in this country, we may have to await a better way to describe them. And in the meantime, we could embark on the interesting thought experiment of calling Arnold Schwarzenegger's pixilated fourteen-year-old his child.

The Perfect Parent

Last year, a friend of mine sent a shipment of green rubber flooring, at great impractical expense, to a villa in the south of France because she was worried that over the summer holiday her toddler would fall on the stone floor. Generations of French children may have made their way safely to adulthood, walking and falling and playing and dreaming on these very same stone floors, but that in no way deterred her in her determination to be safe. This was, I think, an extreme articulation of this generation's common fantasy: that we can control and perfect our children's environment. And lurking somewhere behind this strange and hopeless desire to create a perfect environment lies the even stranger and more hopeless idea of creating the perfect child.

Of course, for most of us, this perfect, safe, perpetually educational environment is unobtainable; a casual fantasy we can browse through in *Dwell*, or some other beautiful magazine, with the starkly perfect Oeuf toddler bed, the spotless nursery. Most of us do not raise our children amidst a sea of lovely and instructive wooden toys and soft cushiony rubber floors and healthy organic snacks, but the ideal exists and exerts its dubious influence.

This fantasy of control begins long before the child is born, though every now and then a sane bulletin lands amidst our fashionable perfectionism, a real-world corrective to our overarching anxieties. I remember reading with some astonishment, while I was pregnant, a quiet, unsensational news story about how one study showed that crack babies turned out to be doing as well as non–crack babies. Here we are feeling guilty about goat cheese on a salad, or three sips of wine, and all the while these ladies lighting crack pipes are producing intelligent and healthy offspring. While it's true that no one seemed to be wholeheartedly recommending that pregnant women everywhere take up crack for relaxation, the fundamental irony does appear to illustrate a basic point: that children, even in utero, are infinitely more adaptable and hardy and mysterious than we imagine.

And yet the current imagination continues to run to control, toward new frontiers and horizons of it. A recent book generating interest in the United States is called *Origins: How the Nine Months Before Birth Shape the Rest of Our Lives*. It takes up questions such as whether eating more fish will raise the intelligence of your child, or what exact level of stress is beneficial to the unborn child. (Too much stress is bad, but too little stress, it turns out, is not good either. One doctor reports that she has pregnant women with blissfully tranquil lives asking her what they can do to add a little healthy stress to the placid uterine environment.)

Then, just last month came a well-publicized British study that suggested that a little drinking during pregnancy is healthy, and that children whose parents drank a little bit were, if anything, slightly more intelligent than children whose mothers refrained from drinking entirely. One might think this new evidence would challenge the absolutism of our attitudes about drinking and pregnancy, the quasi-religious zeal with which we approach the subject, but it's equally possible that it won't have much effect. Our righteousness and morally charged suspicion that drinking even the tiniest bit will harm an unborn child runs deeper than rational discussion or science; we are primed for guilt and sacrifice, for the obsessive monitoring of the environment, for rampant moralism and reproach, even before the baby is born.

One of my friends asked me, very sensibly, "Is it worth even the smallest risk?" about a glass of wine late in my pregnancy, and of course the answer has to be no. What kind of Lady Macbeth would place her own fleeting if urgent desire for a glass of wine above her child's health, or ability to get into an excellent college? However, the question itself betrays its own assumptions: our exaggerated vision of risk and sensitivity to the impossible idea of control may also be damaging to a child.

If you drink a little, the popular logic goes, your child might be a little dumber. He won't be damaged per se, but he'll be a little dumber. Behind this calculation is the mystical idea of engineering the perfect child. But perhaps the question we should be asking ourselves is, Even if we can engineer him, will he grow up to be unbearable?

You know the child I am talking about: precious, wide-eyed, over-cared-for, fussy, in a beautiful sweater, or a carefully hipsterish T-shirt. Have we done him a favor by protecting him from everything, from dirt and dust and violence and sugar and boredom and egg whites and mean children who steal his plastic dinosaurs, from, in short, the everyday banging-up of the universe? The wooden toys that tastefully surround him, the all-sacrificing, well-meaning parents, with a library of books on how to make him turn out correctly—is all of it actually harming or denaturing him?

Someone I know tells me that in the mornings, while making breakfast, packing lunches, and laying out clothes, she organizes an art project for her children. An art project! This sounds impossibly idyllic—imaginative, engaged, laudable. And yet, is it just the slightest bit mad as well? Will the world, with its long lines in the passport office and traffic jams, be able to live up to quite this standard of exquisite stimulation? And can you force or program your child to be creative?

The bookshelves offer bright assistance: *Amazing Minds: The Science of Nurturing Your Child's Developing Mind with Games, Activities, and More; Raising Your Spirited Child: A Guide for Parents Whose Child Is More Intense, Sensitive, Perceptive, Persistent, Energetic; Free-Range Kids: How to Raise Safe, Self-Reliant Children (Without Going Nuts with Worry)*. These books, and the myriad others like them, hold out the promise of a healthy, civilized venture, where every obstacle, every bedtime, every tantrum, is something to be mastered like an exam at school.

Can we, for a moment, flash back to the benign neglect of the late 1970s and '80s? To children helping themselves to three slices of cake, or ingesting secondhand smoke, or carrying cocktails to adults who were ever so slightly slurring their words. To those evenings when they were not noticed; they were loved, just not monitored. And, as I remember it, those warm summer nights of not being focused on were liberating. In the long sticky hours of boredom, in the lonely, unsupervised, unstructured time, something blooms; it was in those margins that we became ourselves.

And then, of course, it sometimes turns out that the perfect environment is not perfect. Take, for example, the fastidiousness a certain segment of modern parents enthusiastically cultivates. *The New York Times* recently ran an article called "Babies Know: A Little Dirt Is Good for You," which addressed itself sotto voce to parents who insist that everyone who enters their house take off their shoes, who obsessively wash hands, or don't allow their children on the subway and carry around little bottles of disinfectant. Apparently, there is, from a sensible scientific point of view, such a thing as being too clean; children, it turns out, need to be exposed to a little dirt to develop immunities, and it seems that the smudged, filthy child happily chewing on a stick in the playground is healthier than his immaculate, prodigiously wiped-down counterpart. I like this story because there may be no better metaphor for the conundrum of overprotection, the protection that doesn't protect.

As their children get a little bit older, and slightly beyond the range of constant obsessive monitoring, homework offers parents another fertile opportunity to be involved, i.e., immersed. I can recall my own mother vaguely calling upstairs "Have you done your homework?" but I cannot recall her rolling up her sleeves to work side by side with me cutting out pictures of rice paddies for a project about Vietnam, or monitoring how many pages of *Wuthering Heights* I had read. One mother told me about how her seven-year-old, at one of New York's top private schools, received an essay assignment asking how his "life experience" reflected Robert Frost's line in "The Road Not Taken": "I took the one less traveled by." And of course, that would be a question calling out for the parent writing it herself, since the seven-year-old's "life experience" had not as of yet thrown up all that many roads.

One of the more troubling aspects of our new ethos of control is that it contains a vision of right-minded child-rearing that is in its own enlightened, super-liberal way as exclusive and conformist as anything in the 1950s. Anyone who does not control their children's environment according to current fashions and science, who, say, feeds their kid American cheese sandwiches on white bread, or has a party that lasts until two in the morning, is behaving in a wild and reckless manner that somehow challenges the status quo. The less trivial problem is this: the rigorous ideal of the perfect environment doesn't allow for true difference, for the child raised by a grandparent, or a single mother, or divorced parents; its vision is definitely of two parents taking turns carrying the designer baby sling. Mandatory twenty-four-hour improvement and enrichment, have, in other words, their oppressive side.

A quick perusal of a random calendar for a random Saturday for a random member of this generation's finest parents will reveal shuttling to gymnastics class and birthday parties and soccer, and Feeling Art and Expressing Yourself Through Theater—entire days vanishing into the scheduled and rigorous happiness and enrichment of the child, entire days passing without the promise or hope or expectation of even one uninterrupted adult conversation. (Those who fall a little short can only aspire to this condition of energetic and industrious parenting.)

One sometimes sees these exhausted, devoted, slightly drab parents, piling out of the car, and thinks, Is all of this high-level watching and steering and analyzing really making anyone happier? One wonders if family life is somehow overweighted in the children's direction—which is not to say that we should love them less, or less centrally, but that the concept of adulthood has somehow transmogrified into parenthood. What one wonders, more specifically, is whether this intense, admirable focus is good for the child. Is there something reassuring in parental selfishness, in the idea that your parents have busy, mysterious lives of their own, in which they sometimes do things that are not entirely dedicated to your entertainment or improvement?

I also can't help but wonder if all of the effort poured into creating the perfect child, like the haute bourgeois attention to stylish food, is a way of deflecting and rechanneling adult disappointment. Are these parents, so virtuously exhausted, so child-drained at the end of one of these busy days, compensating for something they have given up? Something missing in their marriage? Some romantic disappointment? Some compromise of career or adventure? One can't help but wonder, in other words, what Tolstoy or Flaubert would make of our current parenting style.

The effort to control is prolonged, too, later and later into the child's life. Colleges in the United States have begun to give parents explicit instructions about when it is time to leave after dropping students off at school, because otherwise they won't. Even at college, even with seventeen- and eighteen-year-olds, these parents are lingering, involved, invested, tinkering; they want to stay, in other words, and control more.

Built into this model of the perfectible child is, of course, an inevitable failure. You can't control everything; the universe offers up rogue moments that will make your child unhappy or sick or brokenhearted. The one true terrifying fact of bringing an innocent baby into the fallen world is that no matter how much rubber flooring you ship to the villa in the south of France, you can't protect her from being hurt.

This may sound more bombastic than I mean to be. All I am suggesting is that it might be time to stand back, pour a drink, and let the children torment, or bore, or injure each other a little. It might be time to dabble in the laissez-faire; to let the imagination run to art instead of art projects; to let the imperfect universe and its imperfect children be themselves.

Whose School Is It, Anyway?

When T. S. Eliot wrote about the cruelest month "mixing memory and desire," he might also have had in mind that this is the season of school admissions in New York City. So as the sooty piles of snow melt into gray puddles, parents obsess over the letters they will and won't receive from the school that will or won't confer on their radiant progeny the blessing of its approval. It seems to be a challenge in this season for even the more sensible parents among us, even those who really do have better things to do, not to fall prey to the prevailing fantasy that if your child is rejected from one of these desirable and enlightened places, he or she will be destined for a life of drug addiction, grand theft auto, or general exile and smoldering mediocrity.

My eighteen-month-old recently had his first school interview. Apparently he sailed through it, though how is somewhat mysterious to me. Especially since he calls all fruits "apples," and sentences such as "Mommy. Moon. Get it" are not necessarily indicative of a huge understanding of the workings of the universe. However, no one is too young for the system, and a small obstacle like language cannot be permitted to get in the way of the judging and selecting and general Darwinian sorting to which it is never too soon to accustom yourself in this city. I have been asked to write recommendations for other one-and-a-half-year-olds for this same lovely school, and have thought of writing, but did not actually write, "He knows a lot about trucks."

You might think it would be enough to be unnaturally occupied with your own children's admissions saga, but you would be wrong: it is also important, in certain circles, to be unnaturally occupied with other people's admissions sagas. Recently at a dinner party a few blocks from my house, someone said that the wife of a well-known man was lying about where their twin boys got into school. The mother of these twins claimed that they had "chosen" a less prestigious school over another, more prestigious school, but someone else "knew for a fact" from a connection in the admissions department of the more prestigious school that they had not got in. This mother, the story went, who had given up working to raise her twins, experienced the school rejection as such a crushing failure that she lied about it. And the person who did the energetic digging and unearthing? I am not sure what her motivation was. Does someone at this dinner party stop to think, "Who have we become?" I think in the corner was a disaffected English father, muttering about the class system, but I wasn't there.

And the admissions process is, for many, only the beginning. There is on the part of certain parents, in certain schools, a slightly unholy fascination with the school. They socialize constantly with the other parents, there are opportunities several times every week to have coffee or drinks with them, there are mixers and potluck dinners and listservs; there is perhaps the tiniest bit of cosmic confusion over who exactly is attending the school: the children who just go there, or the parents who revel and revere and bask in it.

It is interesting that the parents at these schools will be the first to tell you that other private schools are very materialistic, and that the culture of these other schools is truly off-putting, that they would never dream of sending their Finn or Ava to the other schools because they would imbibe the wrong values, and they will very happily recount stories of moneyed excess about these other schools, but their school, and by implication, of course, *they* are not like that. (I won't rehash these stories here, but I have recently heard about a fashionable, progressive Brooklyn private school, in which a birthday party of eleven-year-old girls was taken to Victoria's Secret to buy bras and underwear and then they went back to the Soho Grand Hotel to take pictures of themselves and sleep over. At another Manhattan private girls' school, one resourceful mother hired, for her daughter's *Wizard of Oz*–themed seventh birthday party, actual dwarves to serve the food. This is the kind of story that we are talking about, and they are too numerous and florid to fit here.) These parents decrying the materialistic culture of this other school, saying, "It's disgusting, it really is," might be sitting in their beach house, over a dinner of grilled shrimp and fresh corn, with the live-in, uniformed baby nurse upstairs with the colicky baby. If you, from the outside, are having trouble seeing how their life—with its long summers at the beach, winters in the Caribbean, the sprawling apartment on the Upper East Side, the helpful doorman, the ubiquitous housekeeper, the $1,000 boots from Barneys—is so different in its values and messages from these other, materialistic parents at the other school, we will assume that is a problem with your clarity and understanding.

These same parents will also very quickly point out that their school is "diverse." The reality is that their school, like all the other schools, is a tiny bit diverse. There are a few kids who will trudge a very long way every morning, from another neighborhood, on a scholarship, but the large bulk of the class very much resembles in background the other kids in the class. This is a puzzling word, "diverse," thrown around all the school promotions, into pamphlets and brochures and websites, because if you were truly committed to sending your children somewhere "diverse," would you not be selecting a different school, one that doesn't require almost all of its students to pay tuition that could support several villages in Africa? Or do these parents, to be totally honest, just want a little bit of diversity? If the catalogues were being totally honest about what parents are looking for, would they advertise, say, a soupçon of diversity?

The interesting element of this obsession is that each of these unique and excellent schools seems to be conferring some ineffable quality, not just on its students, but on the parents of these students. In the ten minutes they spend dropping their children off in its hallways, they are seeing some flattering image of themselves reflected back: progressive, enlightened, intellectually engaged.

The most sought-after school in my neighborhood, a famously open-minded and progressive and arty yet very exclusive private school, is conferring a kind of creativity on the parents, so that even if they are bankers or hedge-fund guys, as many of them frankly are, they can tell themselves in the dark of night that they are creative people, because their children attend this

impeccably creative school. And if they are creative people—
that is, people who have somehow made enough money to send
their children to this school, but work in film or music or
advertising—they can congratulate themselves on their creativity, even if they are not, although in a creative profession, exactly creating anything themselves. The secret suspicion that you
might be a hack, a glorified hack, making a rather nice living
doing something fun but not truly living out your fantasy of creating art the way you honestly thought you would be in college,
well, the check you make out to that fancy, creative, open place
you are sending your child to is eloquently arguing otherwise.
They are putting on operas when they are three years old, after
all. They are performing *Hamlet* in the second grade. They are
illustrating Wallace Stevens poems by the time they are six. How
could anyone accuse you of just being a banker, or a music executive, or an Internet guy with good glasses? I have a friend whose
five-year-old attends this school. She and her husband were
pleased that when their daughter had an assignment to write
down what she wanted to be when she grew up she wrote "artist." But when they arrived at the class presentation the next day
they saw that all twenty-two children had put down "artist":
there were no veterinarians, no circus acrobats, no doctors, no
hair cutters. Twenty-two artists in one kindergarten class: the
school, you see, does not play around.

Then there are the schools of more traditional erudition on,
for instance, the Upper East Side. You can console yourself, if
you are a partner in a corporate law firm whose experience of
reading, to be frank, is largely confined to your BlackBerry, that
your daughter is sitting in the well-upholstered library, as the af-

ternoon light flows in from the river, highlighting her Ovid. Or if you are a stay-at-home mother, who is whiling away many hours of the one life God gave you at the gym, and at Jimmy Choo, you can be reassured that your seven-year-old is learning "not just to answer but to question."

Then there is the wise but beleaguered segment of the anxious parental population worrying about admission to the Gifted and Talented public schools, which are free but so rare as to be almost mythical. There is a mysterious, almost dauntingly incomprehensible system that you have to master before even testing your child. And it feels like you could study it full-time for years and not ever understand it, and to make it worse the city, in its wisdom, likes to change these byzantine rules every year or so, so it's that much more impossible to figure out. But if you somehow are yourself Gifted and Talented enough to figure it out, and your child has tested into the top 2 percent of children in the city, if they are classified, officially, as "Gifted and Talented," then you still have to wait to see if they are assigned, or lotteried, into one of the tiny handful of excellent Gifted and Talented schools. This would still, even though they have tested into the top 2 percent of children in the city, be less likely than the camel passing through the eye of the needle, or the people from the other more materialistic school getting into heaven, and this wait is more heartbreaking, since you are not sullied or implicated in the unsavory system of private school admissions that is consuming other people around you.

Someone somewhere in this glittering, impossible city is developing the fantasy, right about now, of moving to a small town in Montana, with faded red barns, and open fields, and a heady stretch of watercolor blue sky, where your children chew on stems of hay, and there is one shingled schoolhouse on the top of the hill, where everyone goes, and a battered old vintage bus to take them there. . . . Unless of course the school in the next town over is a little bit better, a little less structured, and a little more creative.

The Feminine Mystique
on Facebook

If from beyond the grave Betty Friedan were to review the Facebook habits of the over-thirty set, I am afraid she would be very disappointed in us. By this I mean specifically the trend of women using photographs of their children instead of themselves as the main picture on their Facebook profiles. You click on a friend's name and what comes into focus is not a photograph of her face, but a sleeping blond four-year-old, or a sun-hatted baby running on the beach. Here, harmlessly embedded in one of our favorite methods of procrastination, is a potent symbol for the new century. Where have all of these women gone? What, some earnest future historian may very well ask, do all of these babies on our Facebook pages say about "the construction of women's identity" at this particular moment in time?

Many of these women work. Many of them are in book clubs. Many of them are involved in causes, or have interests that take them out of the house. But this is how they choose to represent themselves. The choice may seem trivial, but the whole idea behind Facebook is to create a social persona, an image of who you are projected into hundreds of bedrooms and cafés and offices across the country. Why would that image be of someone else, however closely bound they are to your life, genetically and otherwise? The choice seems to constitute a retreat to an older form of identity, to a time when women were called Mrs. John Smith, to a time when fresh-scrubbed Vassar girls were losing their minds amidst vacuum cleaners and sandboxes. Which is not to say that I don't understand the temptation to put a photograph of your beautiful child on Facebook, because I do. After all, it frees you of the burden of looking halfway decent for a picture, and of the whole excruciating business of being yourself. Your three-year-old *likes* being in front of the camera. But still.

These Facebook photos signal a larger and more ominous self-effacement, a narrowing of worlds. Think of a dinner party you just attended, and your friend, who wrote her senior thesis in college on Proust, who used to stay out drinking till five in the morning in her twenties, a brilliant and accomplished woman. Think about how throughout the entire dinner party, from olives to chocolate mousse, she talks about nothing but her kids. You waited, and because you love this woman, you want her to talk about . . . what? . . . a book? A movie? Something in the news? True, her talk about her children is very detailed, very impressive in the rigor and analytical depth and verve she brings to the subject; she could, you couldn't help but think, be writing an entire dissertation on the precise effect of a certain teacher's pedagogical style on her four-year-old. But still. You notice that at another, livelier corner of the table the men are not talking about models of strollers. This could in fact be an Austen or Trollope novel where the men have retired to a different room to drink brandy and talk about news and politics. You turn back to the conversation and the woman is talking about what she packs for lunch for her child. Are we all sometimes that woman? A little kid talk is fine, of course, but wasn't there a time when we were interested, also, in something else?

The mystery here is that the woman with the baby on her Facebook page has surely read *The Feminine Mystique,* or *The Second Sex,* or *The Beauty Myth,* or DoubleX or Jezebel. She is no stranger to the smart talk of whatever wave of feminism we are on, and yet this style of effacement, this voluntary loss of self, comes naturally to her. Here is my pretty family, she seems to be saying, I don't matter anymore.

I have a friend whose daughter for a very long time wore squeaky sneakers. These sneakers emitted what was to adult ears an unbelievably annoying squeak with every single step she took. I asked my friend once why she put up with the sneakers, and she said, "Because she likes them!" Imagine being in this new generation, discovering with every joyous squeak of your sneakers that Galileo was wrong: the sun is not the center of the universe, you are!

Our parents, I can't help thinking, would never have tolerated the squeaky sneakers, or conversations revolving entirely around children. They loved us as much and as ardently as we love our children, but they had their own lives, as I remember it, and we played around the margins. They did not plan weekend days solely around children's concerts and art lessons and piano lessons and birthday parties. Why, many of us wonder, don't our children play on their own? Why do they lack the inner resources that we seem to remember, dimly, from our own childhoods? The answer seems clear: Because with all good intentions we have overdevoted ourselves to our children's education and entertainment and general formation. Because we have chipped away at the idea of independent adult life, of letting children dream up a place for themselves, in their rooms, on the carpets, in our gardens, on their *own*.

Facebook, of course, traffics in exhibitionism: it is a way of presenting your life, at least those sides of it you cherry-pick for the outside world, for show. One's children are an important achievement, and arguably one's most important achievement, but that doesn't mean that they are *who you are*. It could, of course, be argued that the vanity of a younger generation, with their status postings on what kind of tea they are drinking, represents a worse or more sinister kind of narcissism. But this particular form of narcissism, these cherubs trotted out to create a picture of self, is to me more disturbing for the truth it tells. The subliminal equation is clear: *I am my children.*

Facebook was pioneered for a younger generation, of course. It lends itself naturally to strangers who run into each other at parties and flirtations struck up in bars. Part of what is disturbing about this substitution is how clearly and deliberately it subverts that purpose: this generation leaches itself of sexuality by putting the innocent face of a child in the place of an attractive mother. It telegraphs a discomfort with even a minimal level of vanity. Like wearing sneakers every day or forgetting to cut your hair, it is a way of being dowdy and invisible, and it mirrors a certain mommy culture in which it's almost a point of pride how little remains of the healthy, worldly, engaged, and preening self.

What if Facebook pages are only the beginning? What if next are passports and driver's licenses? What if suddenly the faces of a generation were to disappear, and in their places were beaming toddlers? Who will mourn these vanished ladies and when will Betty Friedan rest in peace?

The Child Is King

If you have ever experienced a dark hour of the soul in the middle of a dinner party, when the men seemed to be talking about something intriguing at the end of the table, while you were deeply immersed in a women's conversation about how to transition from the bottle to the sippy cup, the French feminist Élisabeth Badinter's rousing indictment of our child-centric culture, *The Conflict*, is bound to offer some consolation.

Her very French, rather severe and fascinating book does not pander to readability in the way an American cultural analysis would, but she raises important points about the dangers of what she calls *"L'enfant-Roi,"* or "the child is king," culture, to the hard-won gains of feminism. She describes the blow to our freedom, to work, to expansive ideas of self, delivered by rigid standards of what motherhood should be. She discusses and attacks, among other things: the La Leche League and the pressure to breastfeed, the fad for natural birth, the total abstinence from alcohol during pregnancy, and the stigmatization of women who decide not to have children.

Badinter has referred to herself a "fanatic of clarity"; and at times her commitment to clarity, her desire to overresolve or over–pin down, can be a bit constricting. (I prefer, in my feminist tomes, what Elizabeth Hardwick referred to as Simone de Beauvoir's "brilliant confusion"—that is, the willingness to tolerate enlivening conflicts and complexities.) But Badinter's arguments are provocative and rigorous: she explains the phenomena that we are currently struggling with, the phenomena that lead us to rabidly consume and debate books about Chinese mothering or French mothering, in an effort to rethink or recast or correct our current mode of parenting.

Badinter attributes the current enslavement to our somewhat repressive styles of child-rearing to the fact that women with feminist mothers in the seventies onward have rebelled against their experience of being abandoned, or somehow insufficiently mothered, by their working mothers. She writes that these daughters thought to themselves: "In pursuit of your independence, you sacrificed me as well. You didn't give me enough love, enough care, enough time. . . . The truth is, I was not your top priority and you were not a good mother. I won't do the same with my children." This seems possibly true to me, as a sort of larger, underpinning psychology, but there must be more to it as well.

Why *are* we raising our children in this way? Why have we created this oppressive culture for ourselves? (And of course, for those of us not exactly raising our children this way, we are raising them in the shadow of this way: thinking about it, worrying about it, or flagrantly disregarding it with some consciousness of recklessness, some demoralizing whiff of potential failure.) But why has the dominant ideology of child-rearing veered so radically toward responsibility, sacrifice?

While I was mulling over this question, I was reading the back of some fancy granola that happens to be in my house, and it says: "Happiness isn't found on a clothing tag. We've looked! We find happiness in making healthy choices, getting outside and keeping fit—choices that make us feel better, inside and out." This idea of enlightenment through health—this lively preoccupation or concern with what is healthy over, say, what is fun or vivid or pleasurable—is a larger turn that affects our ideas of motherhood. Doing something unhealthy, or creating an unhealthy environment for a child, is currently so taboo that we are tyrannized by the fear of it: we are almost unable to think in other terms.

In discussing the disheartening toll babies take on relationships, Badinter writes, "A mother cannot allow herself to be consumed by her baby to the point of destroying her desires as a woman." It occurs to me that in some sense, many of the mothers she is talking about are using their children as an escape from the imperatives of romantic life. This elevation and fetishization of the child over the parent's private life is perhaps not always the *cause* of unhappiness, but rather it may be some sort of escape from the pressure to be happy, some flight from the demands of romantic connection. If the child is overwhelmingly central to family life, in all of the much discussed, anti-romantic ways, then you are delivered from the demands of true intimacy, at least for a while; it's a reprieve from the expectation of romantic happiness, which can, of course, be exhausting.

Likewise children deliver us from the pressure of our ambitions, the shadows of our failures. I often think of Geoff Dyer's brutal, bravura passage in *Out of Sheer Rage*. In describing his decision not to have children, he writes, "People need to feel that they have been thwarted by *circumstances* from pursuing the life which, had they led it, they would not have wanted; whereas the life they really want is a compound of all those thwarting circumstances. . . . That's why children are so convenient: you have children because you are struggling to get by as an artist—which is actually what being an artist means—or failing to get on with your career. *Then* you can persuade yourself that children had prevented you from having this career that had never looked like working out." And it actually goes on, and I'll continue to quote it because in its bleakness and cynicism it carries a certain insight, an insight that dovetails nicely with Badinter's condemnation of certain attitudes toward motherhood.

> After a couple of years of parenthood people become incapable of saying what they want to do in terms of what they want to do. Their preferences can only be articulated in terms of a hierarchy of obligations, even though it is by fulfilling these obligations (visiting their in-laws, being forced to stay in and babysit) that they scale the summit of their desires. The self-evasion does not stop there: at some level they are ashamed because they realize that these desires are so paltry as to barely even merit the name of desires and so these feeble desires have to take on the guise of an obligation.

The dark idea here again is that children are the best excuse in the world not to pursue happiness, not to live fully or take risks or attempt the work one loves. The compromises we make are justified, elevated, and transfigured by the fact of children, and this can be a relief. And Dyer's point is interesting in that it is not that children transform vibrant, ambitious, desiring people into juice-box-carrying automatons, but rather that the juice box carrying offers a socially acceptable escape from all that troublesome vibrancy.

But these speculations aside, Badinter's impressive imperative to own one's life, to take rigorous and energetic responsibility, to cast off the silly or cowardly or frivolously domestic ways, seems very appealing, and refreshing and brisk. One wishes at the end not to displease or disappoint her, to live up to her lofty ideals, to really try to inhabit her ennobling vision, though one's two-year-old, the little *enfant-roi,* is calling for a cookie.

PART IV

The Internet, Etc.

One Day at a Time

I like to think of myself as only moderately, ordinarily addicted to the Internet. I don't have an iPhone. I don't have a BlackBerry. I don't have an iPad. I am barely involved with Facebook, and can't stand Twitter. But as I think about sitting down to write a book, I do wonder what it would be like to have uninterrupted hours of work—long, luxurious stretches of time, unbroken by dipping into the Internet, skimming through an article, scanning email, buying groceries. To be working, in other words, like it was 1975. Dylan Thomas once wrote, "The summer talked itself away," and I am a little bit afraid of having to say, some months from now, "The fall emailed itself away."

Hence my resolve: What if I spent the time I was supposed to be working and concentrating, working and concentrating? What if I didn't have the great beguiling luminous territory of the Internet to escape to whenever the sentences got a little slow or tricky?

The semi-revolutionary idea of going offline in a very modest and moderate way seems like a reasonable one. I won't vanish, dysfunctionally, off the face of the earth; I will just check my

email, once a day, for fifteen minutes. I envisage this useful and
not entirely radical experiment lasting a week—which is not,
after all, a huge, unmanageable eternity.

A man I meet at a party tells me about a software program
called Freedom. It asks you how long you would like to be offline
(i.e., free) and you tell it, and then it disables your computer so
you can't get on to the Internet for that time—or, in its words:
"Freedom locks you away from the internet." If you should suddenly need to go on the Internet, you can restart your computer
and disable the program, but it offers that extra bit of resistance;
it is the superego, the self-control that you don't quite have. The
name of the program has to be part of its success; it plays on our
hidden desires, the better self we are hoping for, links the program in our heads to revolutions, Arab Springs, Thomas Jeffer-
son. And yet the name also pleasantly and politely hints at another
word: "enslavement." What is frightening is the lack of control
implied by this program, the total insufficiency of will when it
comes to the Internet. Its generally upbeat vibe gestures toward a
certain underlying desperation. I particularly like its slightly Or-
wellian formulation on the website: "Freedom enforces freedom."

I agree with the man at the party that this seems in many ways
exactly what I need, and yet, somehow (and this may be stubborn
and unreasonable and unmodern of me), freedom seems like
something I should not have to buy and download. (There is also
a less intense version of the Freedom program, called Anti-
Social, which disables your email but allows you onto the Internet. And again, I feel that if I am going to be antisocial, I should
be able to do it on my own.)

Of course, the very existence of a program like Freedom,

which outsources discipline and restraint, reveals that these portals, these openings, these trivial little chances to slip into another world are an addiction. They are as powerful an escape in their own way as a couple of cocktails at the end of the day were to another generation, and probably no healthier.

The inventor of Freedom, Fred Stutzman, told a *New York Times* reporter, "We're moving toward this era where we'll never be able to escape from the cloud. I realized the only way to fight back was at an individual, personal level." This sweet-looking, bearded, former information and library science graduate student, whose picture of himself on his website has him carrying a baby in a BabyBjörn, is using the language of battle, the idiom of war. The question is who we are fighting if not ourselves?

Freedom from distraction may be the new, sought-after bourgeois luxury. In his essay "The Joy of Quiet," Pico Iyer says that the future of travel lies in "black hole resorts" where you pay exorbitant amounts for remote beautiful rooms that are offline. The principle is that freedom from the Internet is so rare and exotic and impossible that it is becoming a commodity: it's not iPhones or iPads we have to worry about buying, but peace from them.

I don't generally go in for hysterical visions of technology, but when you start to think about it, the ubiquity of screens, the incessant escape from one place into another, the secret passageway of iPhones and BlackBerrys, the glazed, ubiquitous expression I-am-here-but-I-am-not-here, is a little unseemly. It begins to seem like we don't use the Internet; it uses us. It takes our empty lives, our fruit fly attention spans, and uses them for its infinite glittering preoccupations. Say your train of thought, as you are reading to your baby, goes something like this: "Goodnight moon. Goodnight cow jumping over the moon. J.Crew summer sale 20% off, can you turn in the piece by Friday? Apologies, xx, should we meet at 6:00 at your place? Goodnight bears. Goodnight chairs." This moment suddenly seems to contain within it the entire decline and fall of civilization, or, at the very least, is a little unfair to the baby. Though perhaps he understands. My own baby, for instance, loves screens with such a great consuming passion that he has already torn two computer keys off two different keyboards.

DAY 1

At first I am edgy, jittery, like I need something to do with my hands. I guess this is what withdrawal feels like. I remind myself that there is nothing interesting on my email. But the problem is not that I am waiting for a specific email, but rather the feeling of being connected, the cosmic buzz of being available to the world, the open line to anyone; it's not, in other words, the content that matters, but the state itself. And this is what is alarming to me, because I do sort of harbor the retrograde idea that I should occasionally be in the room with the people I am in the room with (or the book, or the piece of work, or the thoughts in my head).

I am basically experiencing the uneasiness of city people in the country, where the quiet, the lack of ambient street noise, is unsettling, where they are literally thinking, "Where are the sirens, the couple arguing, the car radio, the truck engine?" All the mundane, trivial noise that you always want to block out is suddenly missing, and the crickets or cicadas or birds are only drawing attention to how unnaturally still it is, and how far away you are from civilization.

Here is my computer, here is a stack of books piled next to me, here is a cup of coffee, here is the sun streaming into the parlor windows—ideal working conditions, some might say, and yet I haven't opened a document. It occurs to me that maybe this experiment isn't excellent for my concentration, as I am concentrating mostly on not going online. And then I think about how easy it is to check your email. Just one click, and no one is looking. I think to myself, "No one will know, and it will just be this one time."

I am suddenly desperately, helplessly consumed with the need to order diapers online, and check the front page of the paper, find a map for the restaurant I am going to for dinner, look at the weather for the next ten days, the hourly weather for today; and then there is the intriguing prospect of email, and then, when I look up, two hours have passed. . . . I see now why one writer I talked to goes upstate, where his coverage is spotty, so he can't go on the Internet. I remember suddenly that I wrote my entire last book in a cubicle in the New York Public Library, without wireless. There may be no hope for me. At the end of the day I pretend to myself that I was not actually cheating. I tell myself that it takes a little longer to get used to the idea than I thought, and that the suddenness of going offline in one day was too ambitious and, ultimately, not constructive.

DAY 2

I admit to myself that I am cheating. I am actually like an addict sneaking off to the roof for a cigarette, cheating. After spending a long, guilty stretch checking my email, I go on Facebook. One of my Facebook friends is a stylish and subversive woman who likes to put up pictures of monkeys, with captions like "so much awesomeness" or, about another surrounded by monkeys, "Mr. Popular." She has no children, and is satirizing the way other people post pictures of their babies. For a moment, I appreciate the satire, the metacommentary, and her own ever stylish relation to ordinariness, and then I am disgusted with myself, with Facebook, and with the awesome monkeys.

DAYS 3 & 4

It's the weekend, and so I am not confronted with the computer screen, with the emptiness at the heart of things, with my total inability to deal with solitude, because there are people around all the time.

DAY 5

I am not actually cheating today, but things feel sort of flat, sort of barren. It is not that my email is that exciting, but that there is always the possibility that something exciting will arrive, and it is the possibility that is hard to surrender. What am I missing? It's the highly theoretical connection to everyone under the sun. There is an enforced quality to my work, like I am working, but in a clean, well-lit jail. Actually, this feels less like freedom than www.macfreedom.com.

DAY 6

I look up at the time and notice that I have been working for hours without remembering the sacrifice of the Internet; I am not feeling it beckoning me; I am not feeling restless, or experiencing the nagging sensation "Where is everybody?" This is more like an almost drugged calm, like I imagine other, healthier people feel after yoga. The hours go by and I don't miss the newspaper, or the world, or the invitation to a party. I am working. Finally: uninterrupted.

DAY 7

I feel the reclusive, perfect, pleasurable peace I imagine in someone who has gone to an ashram by the Ganges. If Virginia Woolf were alive in this century, she might have added that to truly concentrate you need £500 and a room of your own, without wireless. I am alone with my thoughts, and somehow don't feel alone with my thoughts. I don't miss the hum of connectedness. But then, of course, at the end of the day, the gold light in the maple outside my window, I do think to myself that it has been a week, and there's no need to be obsessive, or overly dramatic, or excessively misanthropic, and just one click won't hurt . . .

Twitter War

The other morning I woke up to several emails saying "Sorry about Mrs. C." or "Don't worry about Mrs. C." I was not worried about Mrs. C., since I had no idea what they were talking about. I did know that Mrs. C. was the wife of a famous novelist.

By the time I finish my coffee I have a dozen messages—"Wow. Mrs. C."—and soon people I haven't talked to in a decade are messaging me on Facebook, "What's up with Mrs. C.?" I get the sense that Mrs. C. is saying something about me on Twitter when a neighbor stops on the street to tell me that he saw Mrs. C. retweeted by someone else.

Indeed, it's beginning to seem like everyone I have ever stood next to in an elevator suddenly harbors a great desire to talk to me about Mrs. C. They want to hear what I have to say about Mrs. C. How do I feel about Mrs. C.? The only thing I know for sure, by this point, is that half of New York City is very closely following the Twittered moods of Mrs. C.

I had written a long piece on sex and the American male writer that had briefly touched on Mr. C.'s work, a year ago, but other than that I did not know Mrs. C. Apparently another piece I wrote had reminded Mrs. C. of that piece I wrote a year ago. Someone somewhere across the world is fomenting a revolution against a repressive regime on Twitter, but Mrs. C. is a little cranky about her Sunday paper.

Later I come across an article in a New York newspaper: "Mrs. C. and Katie Roiphe in Twitter Battle." A Twitter battle! Wouldn't this be a better battle if I were, say, on Twitter? (I do technically have a Twitter account that I have never once used. That Twitter account was set up by my seven-year-old, who set up her own account, @icoolirock, and then set up mine so that she could have a follower, since I don't let her have strangers following her, meaning, basically, that her love for certain floppy-haired boy singers will have to remain, for now, a secret from the world.)

Soon news of the battle between me and Mrs. C. seems to have spread to other websites: Mediabistro, TheAtlantic.com, NPR.org, NewYorker.com, SFBayAreaObserver.com, The Awl. Even I am not interested enough in Mrs. C.'s tweets to actually read them, and yet here they are spreading across the Internet. A slow news day, maybe?

What I found most intriguing is the question of why remote acquaintances would be interested in calling Mrs. C. to my attention. Many things may have happened in the intervening decade since I had spoken to them, but none had awakened in them the sudden desire to talk to me the way Mrs. C.'s vicious tweeting did. I've noticed the same phenomenon with a scathing review: people who are not my friends suddenly emerging to sympathize, to hear what I think or how I feel about my scathing review. Here, of course, is schadenfreude at work. This is a nervous city, after all, and we like a little of someone else's downfall with our morn-

ing latte and paper. Of course, this illicit pleasure in other people's setbacks is nothing new; in his beautiful 1961 essay, "The
Black Boy Looks at the White Boy," James Baldwin writes about
the "bottomless, eerie aimless hostility that characterizes almost
every bar in New York," with people putting other people down
out of "spite, idleness, envy, exasperation."

But clearly the "bottomless, eerie, aimless hostility" he is talking about is not only floating around bars and parties these days,
but on the Internet. The nasty rumors, the lies, the blatant attacks, the vengeance circulating, the trivial and contentless nastiness breeding more, the jealousy, vanity, thwartedness finding
expression. Would Mrs. C., if she ran into me at a bar, confront
me, or maybe throw a drink at me? I would say probably not
(though Mrs. C. may be a bit volatile, so I can't be sure).

Of course, Mrs. C. has every right to express her opinions,
and distant, long-lost acquaintances have every right to call them
to my attention, in the spirit of concern or general curiosity or
whatever mysterious motives animate people in tiny little moments like these. But it does make me wonder whether schadenfreude has a healthy new life on the Internet, the shadow city at
war with itself.

The future of schadenfreude? I don't know. I'll have to con-
sult with @icoolirock.

The Language of Fakebook

I have a feeling that if Andy Warhol were alive he would be spending the summer writing a novel that takes place in real time on Facebook. In that spirit, Lauren Mechling and Laura Moser have been writing a clever serialized novel on Slate called *My Darklyng*. Their innovation: the plot unfolds not just in text but on Facebook and Twitter.

For the purposes of what they affectionately call their "gonzo art project," the veteran young-adult novelists Ms. Mechling and Ms. Moser created a fake Facebook page for their main character, sixteen-year-old Natalie Pollock. What's fascinating is that Natalie's page may seem fake and stilted and artificial, but only in the way all teenagers' Facebook pages seem fake and stilted and artificial.

Which is to say "My Darklyng" offers a brilliant commentary on how fictional teenagers are on Facebook. Their stylized, mannered projections of self are as invented as any in a novel. There are regional differences, of course, to the mannerisms, but there are certain common tics: Okayyyyyyyyy. Ahhhhhhh. Everything is extreme: So-and-so "is obsessed with." So-and-so "just had the longest day EVERRRRRR." They are in a perpetual high pitch of pleasure or a high pitch of crisis or sometimes just a high pitch of high pitch. Holden Caulfield might have called it "phoniness."

A fourteen-year-old I talked to about this sent me a message that pretty much sums it up: "I write more enthusiastically on Facebook than I actually am in real life. Like if I see something remotely funny I might say 'HAHAHAHAHAHAHAHAHA-HAHAHAHAHAHHA,' when really there is no expression on my face."

Another girl tells me she spends one, or maybe three, or maybe six hours a day on Facebook. She gets updates and messages to her phone during the school day, when she is not on summer vacation, hanging out on Facebook the way some people in a quaint and distant era might have hung out at a pool. It would be hard to say exactly how much time we are talking about, but suffice it to say: it's a lot of time.

In the dark, medieval days before the Internet, teenagers were forced to scribble their stagiest experiments in selfhood in journals and notebooks, or to express themselves through their clothes. The high drama was the same, the amped-up, overstated processing of life the same, but the media available were inferior. How amazing to be able to tell your 1,344 closest friends, "Guess who I saw at the Apple store? I died it was so awkward!!!!!!!" Or "I am so freaked out and excited about tomorrow I can't stop eating, are you experiencing this?" or "Robert in twilight is so ahhhhhhhhhhhhh." Facebook gives the exhibitionism, the pure theater, of those years a whole other level of stage.

In "My Darklyng"'s intriguing metacommentary, there is a certain cross-pollination of what might be considered real life and fiction. Ms. Mechling and Ms. Moser hired a fifteen-year-old, Hannah Grosman, to be featured in photographs and videos for the character Natalie's Facebook page. There are real people commenting on Natalie's page; Hannah uses one of the photos from a photo shoot of herself as Natalie with another actress as the profile picture on her real Facebook page. A video of a kiss at the World Cup was posted on Natalie's page just minutes before one of Hannah's real friends posted the same thing. So it is no longer art imitating life, or life imitating art, but the two merging so completely, so inexorably, that it would be impossible to disentangle one from the other, rather elegantly making the point that these media, YouTube, Twitter, Facebook, all this doodling in the ether, involve wholesale inventions of self, not projections.

One predominant fictional argot of Facebook for teenagers would be breathlessness or emphatic speech. Their pages are peppered with "Okkkkayyyyy" and "HAHAHAHA" and "OMG!!!!!" You can find polite little girls cursing like sailors on Facebook. Everything is louder, more ardent, capitalized. This is a way of dramatizing or raising the stakes on even the most inane or banal exchange: You don't just look cute. You look sooooooooooooooo cute!!!!!!! For every piece of idle communication it is as if you are stranded on a desert island, waving your arms and jumping up and down to get the attention of a passing plane.

One of the other great adolescent poses of Facebook is irony at all times. So if you say, "Can't wait for the Lady Gaga concert," you might add "lol," or you might say, "Hey you are at camp and I'm in England, but I just wanted to let you know that I miss youuuu hahaha," to make it clear that you are not really looking forward to anything or expressing an actual emotion in a way that might be overly earnest or embarrassing.

Many, especially slightly older, teenagers seem to like to parody the Facebook norms even as they embrace them. The idea is that you are pretending to speak in the common language of Facebook, and are in fact speaking in that common language, but are aware of how unoriginal you are being; so when you write "omg" you are ironically commenting on the use of "omg," but when other people write "omg" they are seriously saying "oh my God." This very delicate balancing act is artful, in its way. Your character is now employing the clichés of the genre, but with satire, or maybe that would be satirrrrrrrrrre.

It is, in short, a brilliant stroke to use Facebook for novel writing, because in general Facebook feeds on fiction; it consumes it, and spits it out in every direction.

Being "friends" on Facebook is more of a fantasy or imitation or shadow of friendship than the traditional real thing. Friendship on Facebook bears about the same relation to friendship in life as being run over by a car in a cartoon resembles being run over by a car in life. Facebook is friendship minus the one-on-one conversation, minus the moment alone at a party in a corner with someone (note to ninth graders: chat and messages don't count); Facebook is the chatter of a big party, the performance of public cleverness, the façades and fronts and personas carefully crafted, the one honed line, the *esprit de l'escalier;* in short, the edited version. Do you know anything at all about your Facebook friends? Do you, in spite of the "misssssssssss you girlieeeee!!!!!" and the "I canttttttt believe you are going awayyyyyyyyyy," care about all of them? Facebook's chief executive, Mark Zuckerberg, has framed the mission of Facebook in terms of helping "tell the story of your life."

It should be said that adults are not necessarily less fictionalized, or more themselves, on Facebook; they are simply less natural, less conversant, less in their element, when they fictionalize. How many people do you know who are in the midst of some great existential or marital crisis, but whose Facebook page is all family photos from the south of France, or the Vineyard, or Bangkok, and charming things their children said?

Somewhere in the gap between status posting and the person in their room at night is life itself. So fiction is the right response, the right commentary, the right point to be making about who we are in these dangerously consuming media, in these easy addictive nano-connections.

It is not, alas, *The Sun Also Rises*, but Facebook is the novel we are all writing.

The Angry Commenter

A new species has risen from the shallows of the Internet: the angry commenter. Sure, there is a long tradition of inspired cranks and interested retirees who have always written letters to the editor, but something in the anonymity and speed and stamplessness of the Internet has unleashed a more powerful and uncontrolled vitriol. I am not here talking about the thoughtful, intelligent comments, which also abound, but rather the bile unloosed, flashes of fury and unexamined rage that pass as "comment."

The commenter is justifiably angry at the encroachment on his time by the offending article. After all, since he has been tied down with rope and physically forced to read the article all the way to the end, this resentment is justified. "Why do we read this kind of drivel?" one commenter asks, and that would pretty much be the question that suggests itself. Why not just put it down, walk away? (As one non-angry commenter puts it, "The Internet is big. Go somewhere else.") We can only conclude that there must be part of the ritual that the angry commenter enjoys, some small thrill in hating something and being able to voice how resentful he is of the precious time that article has robbed him of.

Now, it's easy to see how one might disagree with or dislike an article, but what is more bewildering and bears examination is the response of *hating the writer's guts*. One would think, reading some of these comments, that the writer has done something to the commenter, that there has been some deep personal transgression. One suspects one thing the writer has done is be the writer, and the commenter feels unfairly ghettoized in the comments section, and feels secretly, well, not so secretly, that she should be writing the article, and the *writer* should be commenting. Like, let her see what it's like to be tied down and forced to read an article from beginning to end.

There are several common fantasies about the writer that fly through comments sections. One is that the writer is "privileged," and/or getting rich off of the insipid and offending article. The confidence and specificity of this fantasy is interesting. One commenter claims that a writer "typifies the white, middle-upper class man who attends Harvard. . . . This is because of his race and class privilege. To him, no one really has access to the 'old boys' network' or is thinking too much about jockeying for social position. That's because he is a de-facto member of the old boys' network and already has his social position." One Slate commenter asserts that a writer "can afford to work only sporadically"; another asserts that she "pulled herself up by her manolo blahnik bootstraps," and yet another that the article is enabling her to put more polish "on her Mercedes." Assuming the commenter does not live next door to the writer and is not the writer's sister or best friend, one wonders a little how the commenter is quite so confident about the content of the writer's bank account. Especially since most freelance writers for places like Slate are not exactly paying the rent on the penthouse off their efforts. If the writer has come from a place of privilege—and as in the rest of the world, some have and some haven't—they are most likely frittering away whatever they do have by entering an insecure and unlucrative profession like writing. These demographic realities, though, make little impression on the angry commenter, who, one notes admiringly, sticks to her guns.

We are clearly in a season of class war, and one can understand the class war against a hedge-fund guy, but a *writer*? This is, in other words, a class war Mao or Ho Chi Minh could get behind. In fact, it's possible that Mao or Ho Chi Minh living today would *be* angry commenters.

It's also interesting that the angry commenter comes fairly equally from the right, from the left, and from some other apolitical place of rage. Though I haven't admittedly done a scientific study, it's my impression that angry commenters are a little harder on women writers than male writers, for reasons I am not sure of, though angry commenters themselves are both male and female.

One of the offshoot pleasures of angry commenting seems to be getting angry at the other angry commenters. There is an element of what one might call socializing, a sort of happy hour of nastiness and sniping. Is this joyful little flash of human friction and fraternizing the best they can hope for? As one non-angry commenter writes to some other angry commenters: "I'm sorry your life is so empty that you find it necessary to try and pick fights with random strangers on the Internet."

This raises the question of whether the commenter is basically normal in her daily life. Maybe she is a schoolteacher who is sweet to kindergartners during the day, and then on a Sunday afternoon secretly releases her anger at the unsuspecting world? Is the person who writes "Move out of the city—seriously— there are too many of you idiot—think you are so sophisticated and special—narcissistic personality disordered yahoos already here I could puke" perfectly polite to the old lady blocking his way in a drugstore aisle? My guess is that the angry commenter is functional, loving, and peaceable in his daily life, and it is only in the comments section that his darkest fury is unleashed (though I could be wrong). In this model one could argue that comments sections are fulfilling an important social function, a kind of collective unconscious that allows the commenter to voice and play out their worst impulses so they can be civilized in their actual lives.

It is possible, though, that there is just more bitterness out there than we realized before the Internet brought us closer to people's rawest, quickest, uncensored thoughts. (That rooting around for a stamp, the walk to the mailbox through the fresh air, the name at the bottom of the letter, did seem to have a mitigating effect on expressions of blind hatred.)

Of course, I am all for everyone's right to express themselves (though it can be more effective to spell and use words correctly). Snobbism is actually one of the commenters' favorite bugaboos, and it is considered snobbish among many angry commenters to prefer that words be spelled or used correctly, spelling and standard written English being a construct of the wealthy, and anyway kind of a show-offy part of the writer's "privilege." We all do have spell-check on our computers, so clearly if the angry commenter wanted to, she could spell correctly too, but spelling correctly would be giving in to the whole hierarchy, namely the idea that some things might be more interesting to read than other things, that has angered her in the first place.

Anyway, the angry commenter is a new breed, and the study of them also new: I welcome, of course, any further evidence or information that would help our understanding of this fascinating and mysterious species.

Gawker Is Big Immature Baby

One bright day a book came across my desk with a letter from its editor saying that the writer was a "big fan" of my work and would like a blurb. As the writer was from Gawker, it seemed a tiny bit surprising that she would be "a big fan" of my work as Gawker itself is not a big fan of my work, and in fact a quick search turned up an item by this writer called "Katie Roiphe Is Big Immature Baby." Admittedly I did not find this piece very wounding, but some old-fashioned part of me still found it strange that she would send me her book for a blurb. I thought if I had written "Joan Didion Is Big Immature Baby," I would probably not send a book to her for a blurb.

But then it occurred to me that perhaps I had misunderstood Gawker. If you are pumping out autopilot schadenfreude all day long, maybe there is nothing personal in it. The rage, the dissociated nastiness, floats through the ether and attaches itself fleetingly to a subject, but really, taking it personally is like being annoyed at the wind for messing up your hair. The attack is so generalized, so mindless, so contentless, why would the writer think I would attach any specific animus to it, or that it was in any specific way intended for or directed at me?

Here I suppose is my main objection to Gawker: it's all tone, no content, and the tone itself is monotonously unvaried— namely the sneer. (Of course, fans and devotees of Gawker might argue that I am exaggerating and there is a full, impressive range of tone that goes all the way from smirk to sneer.) What the Gawker ethos (i.e., the sneer) comes down to is this: everyone is a phony, except presumably those writers at Gawker who labor tirelessly to point out this phoniness (think Holden Caulfield gone a little sour, and getting a little old).

Gawker takes the explicit stance of the outsider, specifically the fashionably slothful outsider. They once republished a piece about one of my essays: "I think she wrote the piece because she liked the idea of having a big, long, 'provocative' think piece in the NYTBR, one lots of people would argue about. I don't blame her for that. If I had my shit more together, I'd probably aim for the same brass ring of neediness." In other words, they murmur to their reader: I am brilliant and talented, but too cool or sub- limely untainted by anything as sordid and uninteresting as the ambition to try to do anything.

I imagine on a good day the producers of Gawker feel that they are serving a function: keeping people honest. But the high- est form of keeping people honest demands more wit, more pre- cision, more specificity, more sharpness. If you make fun of everyone in the same register, in the same tone, it begins to be a little generic. ("Jesus Christ, Bill, you're hogging a media plat- form that could be used to say something, you know, interest- ing.") The idea that you could almost plug in anyone to the formula is almost explicitly part of Gawker's approach ("Frank

Bruni is the new Bill Keller is the new Thomas Friedman! Which is to say, the latest New York Times columnist who can be reliably depended upon to use his priceless media real estate to write utterly vacuous and worn-out tripe.")

It's not that one wants one's gossips to be nice, exactly, but one wants them nuanced, substantive. One wants to remember an amazing line, and not have a vague impression of cloudy nastiness. Think of great or colorful or stylish pieces of nastiness that stay in your head. Take, for instance, what other writers made of Mary McCarthy's smile. Susan Sontag wrote, "Mary McCarthy can do anything with her smile, even smile with it"; Dwight Macdonald said in an interview, "When most pretty girls smile at you, you feel terrific. When Mary smiles at you, you look to see if your fly is open"; Randall Jarrell wrote of his McCarthy character in a novel, "Torn animals were removed at sunset from that smile." Or think of Virginia Woolf describing a visit with T. S. Eliot "in his four-piece suit." Or Nabokov observing that some of his students' ears were "merely ornamental."

Humor, and even name-calling, are more effective when they're less generic, less anonymous, less generally applicable to anyone who has done anything. I can speak to this as a target: more effective than "Katie Roiphe Is Big Immature Baby" or even Gawker's poem in their feature, "Shut Up, Katie Roiphe" is when, in *The New Yorker*, someone once called me a "self proclaimed bad girl and sexual rebel." It had an admirable understated sting, that "self proclaimed." It was saying something specific and interpretive about the book it was skewering, about me. I don't agree with it, of course, but I can see that it was an excellent and effective instance of name-calling.

Of course, one could argue that Gawker is less the real scourge than the gawkerish habits of mind that have been internalized by certain segments of the Internet-scouring populace. To casually and sloppily take down, to ironize, to sneer, comes very naturally to us, we can do it in our sleep, but to care, to try, to want, are harder. And to admit that you care or are trying or are wanting, well, forget it: those will be impossible.

There is a great moment in *Paradise Lost* where Satan is trying to persuade Eve to eat the apple and he says, "These, these, and many more / causes import your need of this fair fruit." He turns his groping, his very inarticulateness, into a style. And it is this mindless rattling of the saber, this contentless argument, this portentous throat clearing, that I think Gawker has, to their credit, perfected: these, these, and many more causes are why you should hate Miranda July or Tom Friedman or Stephenie Meyer.

I gather there are a lot of restless assistants and bored office people who thrive on that secret, inarticulate razzing, that blind grasping at reasons to hate, that vivid stirring of resentment, that rage with nowhere to settle—Stephenie Meyer! No, Miranda July! And I don't think it is a doomed or fruitless venture to draw on the resentment and bitterness and envy adrift in this city. But what would it be like to draw on it with more personality, more artfully? In the end, a computer program could produce Gawker, which is why it doesn't matter which of their writers pens an item, or if an old one leaves or a new one comes, or if one of them would like to disassociate herself because she would like a blurb for a book.

I suppose what is disheartening or surprising is not that the city's disappointed artists or thwarted hopeful or anxious young love Gawker, but that there isn't a better Gawker for them to love.

Whiplash Girlchild in the Dark

I write to Alexis because she seems less hemmed in by convention than me. I know that she is less hemmed in by convention than me because in her Facebook profile photo she is standing on a velvet chaise longue in the Chelsea Hotel in a leather corset, fishnet thigh highs, and crazy platforms holding a whip over her head.

But when I meet her in a bar on the Lower East Side, she is in her day clothes, faded jeans, furry Ugg boots, a black sweater, her hands cupped around a mug of mint tea, because she doesn't drink. I am surprised to see an ordinary blond girl waiting a little uncomfortably at a bar.

On Facebook, where I first experience Alexis, her photographs have an astonishing, almost confusing range. She can be childish, stunning, plain, intense, mannish, elegant, terrifying, magnificent, catlike, innocent, angry, Helmut Newtonish, Greek goddess–like, Marilyn Monroe–like, Venus in furs–like, Valkyrie-like; she can have blond hair, black hair, red hair. Someone who sees her photographs says, "She looks like a whole acting troupe."

So to start with: I've never met anyone so much in command of her own image.

Alexis Lass Trbojevic
"I thought how unpleasant it is to be locked out; and I thought it is worse, perhaps, to be locked in." Virginia Woolf
Like • Comment • Share

Her first week at the dungeon Alexis was overwhelmed by what she saw. What she saw was subs being whipped and caned, subs with bloody marks and welts, subs walking on all fours on leashes, subs getting slapped in the face and spat on, subs licking the bottoms of women's shoes, subs in Little Bo-Peep costumes being forced to suck on dildos while the dommes laughed and taunted them, subs being electrocuted with a special device, subs left bound in cages for six or eight hours. She had to remind herself of a line from *The Night of the Iguana:* "Nothing human disgusts me . . ."

When you start, she says, it feels like being thrown into a deep ocean when you don't know how to swim. You are coughing up water, choking, feeling like you are drowning.

She thought of her mother saying that you become brave by acting brave. Though she also thought of other things her mother would say about what she was doing.

In the beginning it was very hard to get the voice of her Upper East Side upbringing out of her head, to separate the flock of preppy Spence girls in their green plaid uniforms, the blocks of doorman buildings and tulip-lined avenues, from the amorphous entity she was beginning to think of as her self. Those first days in the dungeon, wearing latex, whip in her hands, she hears a voice call her trashy, a whore, a loser, but she doesn't know if it's her voice.

Then somewhere she crosses over. The world she has moved into is so extreme, so profoundly and flamboyantly unacceptable, that it frees her from the narrow or confining definitions of a successful life she was struggling with; it's not like failing a little, or not fitting in a little. It's like going to Mars.

The abstractions here are easier to understand than the specifics. By that I mean that if you watch thirty seconds of one of the fetish films Alexis makes, in which a woman steps in stiletto heels on a man's genitals, you will not see Alexis's world as clearly as if you read Susan Sontag's essay on sadomasochism and fascism: "The color is black, the material is leather, the justification is truth, the aim is ecstasy, the fantasy is death."

When Alexis first told her mother what she was doing, her mother said, "Don't come in the house." Alexis's mother was the closest person in the world to her. Alexis said, "Fine, if that's what you want."

In the end her mother let her back into the house. But the break is still there, not visible but there, the break where you find in yourself the ability to walk away from everything you have known; the break is thrilling, liberating, and, as Alexis says, a little like dying.

Alexis describes her mother as a dark, remote, beautiful creature, drinking coffee, smoking long cigarettes, reading her books by dead Russians. "She would probably be the best domme in the world," Alexis says.

Her father is a Serbian émigré, a scientist, an artist. She mentions that he went to L'Ecole des Beaux-Arts in Paris; he showed his paintings in galleries in the seventies; he worked as part of a team of scientists at Mount Sinai Hospital that won a Nobel Prize for their research; he played chess with Bob Dylan.

He was so formal and European when her mother met him that he wouldn't answer the door without a blazer. But he is not shocked by what Alexis does. As a child during World War II he saw human heads carried around on sticks. Instead, he views what she does as "extreme decadence."

Her father's continuing disapproval makes her feel like she is about to run a long and important race and someone is whispering: "You can't do it, you are going to lose, you'll never make it."

Alexis's grandfather was shot by the Nazis in Belgrade during the war. According to family lore, her chain-smoking grandmother, who is like a tank, marched over to the central office and demanded that they write her a letter explaining why they had killed her husband. Apparently she was so tanklike that the Nazis obliged by writing the letter in German, and Alexis's father still has it. It's a very rare and unusual document: the Nazis explaining themselves.

Alexis Lass Trbojevic
Have to paint the brick walls of the new film studio with a mixture of black paint and water (so the brick looks Medieval) and then coat the walls with water sealer . . . the space is 2,000 sq feet. . . . hummm shall I get redbull or starbucks? Which is stronger?
Like · Comment · Share

One of the tricky financial issues that Alexis runs into with her fetish film business is that she can't resist spending money on the aesthetics: she wants a real goat skull for the Viking shoot, or an antique morgue table from the thirties, or the perfect cigarette holder for a film noirish shoot, or an art deco chaise longue, or a side table from a Masonic temple, or a Carolina Herrera vintage Roman gown.

In one of her films a mysterious redhead lies naked on the art deco chaise longue, her bottom half painted gold, her upper body splattered with gold, a delicate 1920s belt around her waist. A man comes to her house for a date, thinking she will be an easy conquest, and she captures him, and puts him in a cage and makes him her sexual slave. The camera pans to his scared face, and then blacks out.

It could be her weakness as a businesswoman that Alexis cares about how her films look more than she cares about cheaply and efficiently delivering the fetish. In fact it seems as if her heart is most unambiguously in painting the sets, in the installation, in the design, in the construction work, in the hunt for costumes and props, in the trips to Home Depot, in the composition, in the look.

Alexis often explains her attraction to sadomasochism in general as aesthetic. "There is something beautiful about the sound of a whip in the dark," she tells me when she is describing her first days in the dungeon. For her there is also something beautiful in the inversion of regular life: the way the men are on their knees, shirtless, small, bent over, and the women are taller.

I begin to notice that Alexis uses the word "aesthetically" when she wants to distance herself from other things that are happening. On the other hand, she *is* truly interested in the aesthetics of sadomasochism, and I can't think of a time when I have seen her when she doesn't have paint under her fingernails.

Alexis Lass Trbojevic
"Sadomasochism has always been the furthest reach of the sexual experience: when sex becomes most purely sexual, that is, severed from personhood, from relationships, from love."
Susan Sontag
Like • Comment • Share

Of course, I want to know why Alexis is drawn into "the Scene." This will not be a question that she answers easily, though she is generous enough to try. In fact she has already told me that this is the very question the Scene is designed to obscure; it is backstage, off-limits, hidden in some box with chains.

"I know no one goes through this world untouched," she says. "But I needed to be touched more."

One day when she was still trying to be an actress, a man came up to her on the street and told her she should be a dominatrix. He said that he was opening a dungeon, and he would like her to come and work for him. She brushed him off, but not before he told her why he had picked her. Something in her walk. He had seen some mannish edge, some unusual confidence, in her walk.

Another time, when she was nineteen, she was in a sex store picking out a studded costume for a role she had in a film, and someone thought she worked there. She didn't understand why. She was wearing a white T-shirt and jeans, but again, someone recognized her, claimed her.

In this version of events, the Scene has chosen her. But Alexis has other versions, like the one where she is an aspiring actress, an artist, a smart, dyslexic, creative girl from the Upper East Side without obvious office skills in an expensive and demanding city, and she accidentally stumbles on an easy way to make a living.

But why *this particular* easy way to make a living? Or maybe a better question is, Why is this particular way to make a living easy for her? Alexis says that she has "anger issues," but she is not sure where they come from.

One day she tells me about a boyfriend she had who was an editor at *The New York Times.* She was drinking then, and one night at Elaine's, for reasons that are obscure to her, she punched him.

Recently she was angry at her current boyfriend for not doing something that he said he would do. There was a whip in front of her, and sort of instinctually she reached for it. He started running. She says, "What could he do? A big, strong man can't grab a whip. That's what's so fascinating; you can decapitate someone with a whip. He was literally running away." She laughs as she tells this story. "Of course I was like, I am sorry I am sorry I am sorry! It's bad. It's like I don't know how else to act."

Some of her anger she attributes to the frustrations of her childhood. She was a dyslexic, wild, imaginative child trying to fit in at Spence, a rigid, highly structured Upper East Side girls' school, where it was still considered important to teach girls to curtsy. There, from a very early age, she would come up with elaborate lies to cover up for her dyslexia, to try to obscure the reasons she couldn't read aloud or fast enough or well enough. She also felt like the slightly poorer, slightly bohemian kid in a school full of rich girls with doormen.

She remembers one day in art class they were making clay figures. Alexis made hers with breasts, and the other girls thought she was strange.

When Alexis was growing up, there were no other children in the house but there were cats. When she was three or four, she remembers going to the birthday party of a classmate, who was a maharajah's grandson. His face was covered in scratches because she had scratched him. "I didn't have siblings," she explains. "I learned to fight from the cats."

Around this same time one of her teachers told her parents that the girls in her class tended to build blocks outward into sprawling cities, and the boys built up into towers, and Alexis built way, way, way up.

"I actually *have* penis envy!" she says.

When I ask her what separates her from the girls in her films, the other dommes and adult actresses she hires, who are not as compelling to watch, she says, "I hit harder."

She tells me she stands behind them and teaches them how to do it, like a tennis instructor.

Alexis Lass Trbojevic
Looking for a used Coffin for my dungeon-film studio . . . any suggestions where to buy one? :)
Like • Comment • Share

Sessions are exhausting because you are managing someone else's fantasy. Alexis describes it as "walking on eggshells upon eggshells." She watches her subs very closely, for a glance averted, a flicker of an eyelid, tension in shoulders, for the slightest alterations in body posture, for signs that she is going too far or not far enough or in the wrong direction. She is intuiting the fantasy from them, almost drawing it out of their bodies, and she has to be fluid, shifting, perfectly responsive. These guys, she says, are about to blow.

What is striking in her description is that it is the *slaves* who sound dangerous. The way she talks about it, it is like there is an explosion that she is working around, managing, navigating, negotiating. She compares it to being with mental patients on a ward without guards.

Alexis describes the sadomasochistic drama as being organized around the idea of *not* facing what there is to face; the whole structure of the fetish replaces any kind of rigorous introspection. She says, "It's like these guys walk in and need surgery, and we are giving them a massage."

If she begins to sense the sub is getting nasty, or the resentment is building too much, or he is starting to go over the edge, or she feels that he is doing something physically dangerous to himself that she doesn't want a part in, she will cut him off. The cut-off sub can become obsessed or controlling, calling and texting a million times, as she puts it, "like a teenage girl."

I ask her if she is ever tempted to laugh at something a sub wants her to do. She says that she is never tempted because for the sub it is too serious, too intense, too intimate. She says that she might laugh before or after, or when telling the story, but she doesn't laugh during.

One day when we are sitting in an upscale white-tiled coffee shop on the Bowery, Alexis goes for just a second into a voice I have never heard before. She is showing me how easy it is to enter the character of Domme Dietrich, which is her dominatrix name. "Now open your tiny little ears," Domme Dietrich is saying. "Open your tiny little eyes." The voice is rich, contemptuous.

"Is it acting? Well, yeah. But to be good at a role, it has to be you. And this one comes very naturally to me." She says, "It's a way to get out my anger, and I don't feel bad for them because I have this six-foot-tall man standing in front of me, and I am like, Poor you. Poor fucking you—I mean, they could get up at any moment and punch me in the face. Game over."

Alexis Lass Trbojevic
What's most beautiful in virile men is something feminine;
what's most beautiful in feminine women is something
masculine. Susan Sontag
Like • Comment • Share

One rainy day over more mint tea, I mention that if I had her particular array of skills and talents, I might be tempted to find a rich sub who would buy me an apartment and come once a week for a session. But for some reason this fantasy doesn't work for Alexis; even the thought of it irritates her. She has trouble taking a check from her investor for her films. She can't stand the idea of being dependent on a man, subjugated in that particular way; even the idea of a rich boyfriend who buys her presents somehow ruffles her, and when, in a former life, she did have rich boyfriends buy her presents, she didn't want them, thinking, "What am I, your doll?" In fact, she likes it that her boyfriend works

WHIPLASH GIRLCHILD IN THE DARK

for her. The possibility of a rich man supporting her is clearly as repellent and unthinkable as what she does would seem to many of the stay-at-home moms sipping eleven-dollar lattes at D'Ambrosios on Madison Avenue.

I ask Alexis how she would reply to an imaginary feminist who argues that she is degrading herself to fulfill male fantasies for money, that she is being exploited, in her latex dishabille, for oppressive patriarchal fantasies.

This is not how she thinks about the power relations in what she does, and she thinks about them a lot. She says that the payments are called "tributes." She sees that money as equalizing the situation, undoing the humiliation a little, delivering back to these men their ego after they have been totally broken down. In some way the tribute or payment restores these bent-over, shirtless, beaten men back to the often exalted place they have in the outside world.

And of course, being dependent on one man's fantasies or whims is different from being dependent on various fairly interchangeable and shifting subs' payments for services rendered. She compares her work sometimes to being a therapist.

One day, by accident, in an email to Alexis I write S + M instead of S & M. She likes this. In fact she likes it so much she thinks I have done it on purpose as some sort of philosophical comment, but I confess that it's just a slip. "It's much more interesting and true," she writes. "S + M = ?"

A psychiatrist I know once described how the lines between sadists and masochists are blurrier than the roles imply, how dommes identify with injured things, how subs identify with aggression, how each is carrying around both sides, no matter how fixed their roles and defined their fetish. It occurs to me this could be why Alexis likes my typo, that she could be a little more S + M than she appears. Or maybe it's just that my accidental formulation has a sort of fun constructive problem-solving feel to it, like there is an answer we can figure out if we stand there at the blackboard long enough.

Alexis Lass Trbojevic
Good Karma Kitty! Tigger is an inspiring cat. He was rescued with severe wounds and has undergone extensive medical care including needing bandages on 3 out of 4 of his burned paws. Despite his difficult life, Tigger pulled through and is almost ready to leave the vet and go to a foster home.
Like • Comment • Share

I begin to notice that whenever Alexis talks about an interaction between humans and animals she identifies with the animal. She tells me a story she once heard from an artist in Boston about a scientist who thought that dolphins were smarter than people, and argued that *humans* should be put in a glass enclosure, and the dolphins should be allowed to swim around and examine them. Everyone thought he was crazy, Alexis says. He also happened to be the scientist who invented the isolation tank. The artist in Boston actually had an isolation tank in his loft, and Alexis is very interested in isolation tanks, or rather in the question posed by isolation tanks: Who are you alone in the water in the dark?

Alexis volunteers for an animal shelter a few times a week,

cleaning cages, petting the cats, some of whom scratch her arms up, they are so "crestfallen," as she puts it, from being caged. She has taken in about sixteen rescued cats who were going to be killed by the city: Voovoo, Dango, Trotsky, Isis, Chairman Mao, Cole, Gracie, Tiger, Drako, Neko, Snow Shoe, Duther, and probably a few more whose names she can't remember. These cats are divided between her dungeon-slash–film studio and her parents' house, in spite of her parents' slightly tepid enthusiasm for the venture. These rescued cats are in addition to her tortoise, her Japanese koi fish, and her three dogs, Shiva, Lulu, and Kuba.

Alexis tells me that taking care of the koi fish and keeping them healthy is like learning chemistry: you have to learn how to delicately balance all of these complicated elements of their environment. She had one called Aiko, who had a sense of humor and did tricks when people were around. "He was like a little dolphin with a little human soul," she says. One day he got sick and she tried to save him, but she couldn't. She still keeps him in her freezer. Sometimes someone will say it's time to bury the fish, but she can't.

Once, right out of college, Alexis had a very brief marriage. She knew it was over because she began to order wild animals over the Internet. For a while she had one wolf and one half wolf running around her apartment on the waterfront in Brooklyn.

Alexis Lass Trbojevic

I only like New York City in the rain if I have a slave to hold an umbrella over my head.

Like • Comment • Share

Alexis has talked to me about the following slaves and subs (when I ask her how she uses these two words, she says "slave" is the more derogatory or slangy word for "sub"): there is the man who wants her to stand above him and drop shoes on him; there is the Scandinavian man she has never met who has a shrine of her photographs in his house, whom she instructs via the Internet, and who sent her money to pay for a coffin for a film shoot; there is the lawyer who she pretends is the only male worker in a shoe factory; there is the Chinese billionaire who wants to be beaten bloody, and was badly abused as a child (she tried to interest him in some other less bloody form of humiliation, but he drifted away, only to come back when she advertised for a sub who wouldn't mind being badly beaten for one of her films); there is the man high up in the Department of Social Services who wants to play the role of an abused child; there are doctors, surgeons, financial guys; there is a descendant of Freud who responded to an ad she posted that quoted Freud saying something like "Only through pain is there consciousness"; there is the man who paid for her to go out to a fancy dinner with her boyfriend so she could text him pictures during the date and show him that she was just using and humiliating him; there is the shadowy English investor who has given her $300,000 to make her fetish films; there are the slaves who come and clean her studio.

Alexis Lass Trbojevic
"Insomnia is an all-night travel agency with posters advertising faraway places." Charles Simic
Like · Comment · Share

Alexis says that she is transitioning out of sessioning, which she rarely does anymore anyway, out of fetish films, into maybe a reality show about the business, into making respectable but still alternative films.

When she talks about the future, she imagines living on an animal sanctuary in upstate New York. She would like to have wolves, giraffes, lions—which, she tells me, you can get special permits for. She would like to have three children, two girls and one boy, two blond and one redhead, and she likes the names Isis and Skull. She tells me that her mother jokes that if she had a child she would leave him outside making a snowman. And then he would be frozen when she finally went out to find him. We both laugh. I think of Goethe's line "Behind every joke there is a problem." Alexis is thinking that same thing. "I guess I'll have to find a man who is kind of like my housewife, who has more maternal or domestic instincts than me."

Alexis Lass Trbojevic
Suzy Sunshine.
Like • Comment • Share

For an angsty dominatrix, Alexis has a straightforwardly warm and beautiful smile. One day she posts a generically pretty blond smiling actress headshot-style photograph, which is startling in the context of her oeuvre. Beneath it, she writes, "Suzy Sunshine," maybe a little embarrassed by the undeniably conventional prettiness of the photo, but the commenters, her Facebook admirers, subs, ex-subs, remote subs, aspiring subs, and other assorted observers, rush toward interpretation. One writes, "Girl next door," and Alexis writes "yuck" and someone else writes, "Dear Alexis is not the girl next door. Anything BUT," and someone else writes, "This kitten bites." and someone else suggests she should model and Alexis says she doesn't want to model. But somehow in the tangle of comments it is clear: everyone, even the most twisted sub, is drawn to the smile.

Another time I see the smile is in a picture she has of herself when she is maybe eight or nine. She is riding her reddish horse, an Arabian mix, Ember. She is lying as flat as she can against her horse's neck, pressing every possible square inch of her body against her, beaming gloriously. Her parents, though not rich, bought her a pony because she loved to ride, and boarded it upstate within walking distance of a train station. In fact her mother put nine-year-old Alexis on the phone to negotiate the price of the horse with the seller. Alexis was especially good with highstrung or difficult horses, which Ember was, because she knew instinctively how to handle them. She says, "I would think to myself, Please let me never never get into boys."

When I watch a few trailers of her fetish films, I am surprised to catch in one of them the smile. Alexis is a cowgirl domme, holding down a slave, while another cowgirl domme is doing things to him, and there's the radiant smile. Is she acting? I can't tell.

Alexis Lass Trbojevic
Mornings feel like someone whispering "fuck you" into your ear . . .
Like • Comment • Share

We are talking about *Story of O,* a famous French novel from the fifties about sadomasochism. I am somehow simultaneously bored and very disturbed by the extremes of how O is transfigured, how she loses herself, how she vacates herself in the course of her baroque sexual enslavement. The novel culminates in a scene where O is wearing an owl mask, and is led on a chain naked into a party, where it occurs to none of the guests that she is human. When Susan Sontag writes about O she talks about "the voluptuous yearning toward the extinction of one's consciousness."

I mention the scene where O is branded and passes out, and Alexis mentions that she once took part in a branding. She was with another domme who had a sub who was a math teacher from Ohio and wanted to be branded. The other domme sent a slave on a long drive to get a blowtorch, and they somehow found a branding iron that said "m." It was just what they happened to find, but they thought maybe "m" could stand for "mistress."

Alexis thought that she could hold the blowtorch because she had done welding before. She was nervous, and the slave was nervous, but she held it steady, the flame blue and red. She stood in a leather bikini and stilettos, holding it very still, while the other domme took the branding iron and put it on his skin, which melted white. After it was over, the dominatrixes started laughing, not a mean laugh, she explains, but nervous, relieved, scared. They had never done anything like that before.

Alexis said to the other domme, "Are you just going to leave him like that?" And the other domme got some Neosporin, and a bandage.

But now she thinks that was going too far; she would never do anything like that again. That was the early stage of her fascination: she was intoxicated by the extremes, she wanted to take things as far as they could go. It was like going to war, you came back and you were desensitized. But now she is done with that. In certain moods, i.e., the one she is in this afternoon, it sounds like she is done with the Scene.

Alexis Lass Trbojevic
Full page foot fetish advert in the New York Times this week.
Like • Comment • Share

One of Alexis's ex-subs is taking her to the play *Venus in Fur* that evening. He is the one who is a descendant of Freud.

I ask her what one wears when going to a play about sadomasochism with an ex-sub; I ask because I have almost never seen Alexis in anything but faded jeans, and today, cat-hair-covered black leggings. The answer is Prada black pants, black blazer, heels. This somehow raises the question in my head of whether the ex-sub still looks at her, and thinks, like the character in *Venus in Fur* looking at his mistress, that she is "half of hell, half of dreams."

At the theater a girl one row behind her gasps out loud when the actress leads a man by a dog collar. Alexis can't believe that the girl is shocked by a dog collar, that she reacts as if the actress has kicked a puppy across the stage.

Afterward, Alexis talks to the Freud descendant about it. He says that people are shocked by the explicit talk about power relations that underlie all relationships: the exaggeration of everyday servitudes and subjugations is what alarms them. This makes me think of a line about couples from the original novel *Venus in Furs*, written in 1870 by Leopold von Sacher-Masoch: "Whichever of the two fails to subjugate will soon feel the feet of the other on his neck."

> Alexis Lass Trbojevic
> Just back from Venus in Furs on Broadway.... the "You don't have to tell me about Sadomasochism" T-shirts were flying off the racks there... interesting... hummm
> Like • Comment • Share

Alexis's dungeon-slash-studio floats above an anonymous midtown street; the dungeon is very clean and well lit and tastefully furnished for a dungeon. Somehow it feels like early morning here, even though it is two in the afternoon. There is a skinny gray cat wandering past the giant wooden cross, and a fluffy black one curled up on the thirties morgue table, and another black one rubbing his back against one of the two mannequins with wigs who are bound together with ropes, and four or five others wandering past the metal wheeling rack for costumes, and one curled up asleep on the low mattress that is there for late nights.

Alexis is tired from staying up until two shooting photographs of a Viking girl covered in silver body paint with a goat skull. Alexis had made her an elaborate helmet with fur, and built and painted a three-dimensional silver rock wall for the background.

In one of the pictures the Viking girl is holding a sword aimed so directly at the camera that you can't quite see what it is.

I think of other people I know with what Alexis calls "anger issues," the way it seeps into and poisons the lives of those around them, in socially acceptable ways, in ways not visible to the outside world, how things happen, minor dramas in the kitchen, books or other objects thrown or torn into pieces, fetishes unnamed and unwanted but still playing themselves out, accidental rituals of humiliation, humdrum or otherwise, little banal stories of O on the subway ride to work, the boring everyday way people "voluptuously yearn toward the extinction of their consciousness," or not even that voluptuously.

The Viking girl already sent Alexis a text this morning saying she is having second thoughts about the topless photos with silver body paint because her fundamentalist Christian family in Texas might see them. Alexis is more or less taking the position that body paint is clothes.

Somewhere in the middle of this, Alexis is telling me about a dinner party she went to with her parents on the Upper East Side, at the house of an important judge. They are sitting around the table, the judge, his wife, his son who goes to an all-boys school, his eighty-five-year-old mother, with dyed red hair, Alexis and her family, and a couple of other Upper East Side friends, eating a pork roast from Lobel's, with horseradish sauce and wine brought back from Italy. They are talking about things they regret not doing. Someone turns politely to the important judge's eighty-five-year-old mother and asks her what she regrets not doing. She says, "I wish I'd been a stripper."

In the dungeon, the window to the fire escape is criss-crossed with bars. Alexis takes another sip of her orange soda and lights a menthol cigarette.

I would like to one day see her at the animal sanctuary, walking with the giraffes, a straw-haired toddler at her ankles, paint still under her nails.

Acknowledgments

Huge thanks and a glass raised to my editors: Noah Eaker, Susan Kamil, Sam Tannenhaus, Jennifer McDonald, Jennifer Schuessler, Laura Marmor, Hanna Rosin, Jacob Weisberg, David Plotz, Meghan O'Rourke, Ann Hulbert, Sue Matthias, Tina Brown, Elissa Schappell, Rob Spillman, Susan Morrison, and Colin Harrison.

"The Great Escape" originally appeared in different form in *New York* magazine.

"The Alchemy of Quiet Malice" originally appeared in different form on Slate.

"Unquiet Americans" originally appeared in different form in *Tin House*.

"Beautiful Boy, Warm Night" originally appeared in different form in *The Friend Who Got Away*.

"The Naked and the Conflicted" originally appeared in different form in *The New York Times Book Review*.

"Writing Women" originally appeared in *The New York Times Book Review*.

"The Bratty Bystander" originally appeared on Slate.

"Reclaiming the Shrew" originally appeared in *The New York Times Book Review*.

"Making the Incest Scene" originally appeared in different form in *Harper's Magazine*.

Parts of "Joan Didion" originally appeared in different form on Slate and in *Brill's Content*.

Parts of "Susan Sontag" originally appeared on Slate and *The New York Times Book Review*.

"The Ambiguities of Austen" originally appeared in *The Weekly Standard*.

"Rabbit at Rest" originally appeared on Slate.

"Do Childish People Write Better Children's Books?" originally appeared on Slate.

"The Perverse Allure of Messy Lives" originally appeared in different form in *The New York Times*.

"The Fantasy Life of the American Working Woman" originally appeared in *Newsweek*.

"Is Maureen Dowd Necessary?" originally appeared on Slate.

"Profiles Encouraged" originally appeared in *Brill's Content*.

"Elect Sister Frigidaire" originally appeared in *Thirty Ways of Looking at Hillary*.

"Love Child" originally appeared on Slate.

"The Perfect Parent" originally appeared in different form in *Financial Times*.

"Whose School Is It, Anyway?" originally appeared in *Financial Times*.

"The Feminine Mystique on Facebook" originally appeared in different form on Slate.

"The Child Is King" originally appeared on Slate.

"One Day at a Time" originally appeared in different form in *Financial Times*.

"Twitter War" originally appeared in different form in *Financial Times*.

"The Language of Fakebook" originally appeared in *The New York Times*.

"The Angry Commenter" originally appeared on Slate.

"Gawker Is Big Immature Baby" originally appeared on Slate.

This book is set in Fournier, a typeface named for Pierre Simon Fournier, the youngest son of a French printing family. He started out engraving woodblocks and large capitals, then moved on to fonts of type. In 1736 he began his own foundry and made several important contributions in the field of type design; he is said to have cut 147 alphabets of his own creation. Fournier is probably best remembered as the designer of St. Augustine Ordinaire, a face that served as the model for Monotype's Fournier, which was released in 1925.